AF306388

Restless justice

Manchester University Press

Series editor

ALEXANDER THOMAS T. SMITH

To buy or to find out more about the books currently available in
this series, please go to: https://manchesteruniversitypress.co.uk/
series/new-ethnographies/

Restless justice

Asylum, homelessness and volunteering

Mark Rainey

MANCHESTER UNIVERSITY PRESS

Published by Manchester University Press
Oxford Road, Manchester, M13 9PL

www.manchesteruniversitypress.co.uk

British Library Cataloguing-in-Publication Data
A catalogue record for this book is available from the British Library

ISBN   978 1 5261 4554 3   hardback

First published 2026

The publisher has no responsibility for the persistence or accuracy of URLs for any external or third-party internet websites referred to in this book, and does not guarantee that any content on such websites is, or will remain, accurate, accessible or appropriate.

EU authorised representative for GPSR:
Easy Access System Europe, Mustamäe tee 50, 10621 Tallinn, Estonia
gpsr.requests@easproject.com

Typeset by Newgen Publishing UK

Contents

Series editor's foreword

When the *New Ethnographies* series was launched in 2011, its aim was to publish the best new ethnographic monographs that promoted interdisciplinary debate and methodological innovation in the qualitative social sciences. Manchester University Press was the logical home for such a series, given the historical role it played in securing the ethnographic legacy of the famous 'Manchester School' of anthropological and interdisciplinary ethnographic research, pioneered by Max Gluckman in the years following the Second World War.

New Ethnographies has now established an enviable critical and commercial reputation. We have published titles on a wide variety of ethnographic subjects, including English football fans, Scottish Conservatives, Chagos islanders, international seafarers, African migrants in Ireland, post-civil war Sri Lanka, Iraqi women in Denmark and the British in rural France, among others. Our list of forthcoming titles, which continues to grow, reflects some of the best scholarship based on fresh ethnographic research carried out all around the world. Our authors are both established and emerging scholars, including some of the most exciting and innovative up-and-coming ethnographers of the next generation. *New Ethnographies* continues to provide a platform for social scientists and others engaging with ethnographic methods in new and imaginative ways. We also publish the work of those grappling with the 'new' ethnographic objects to which globalisation, geopolitical instability, transnational migration and the growth of neoliberal markets have given rise in the twenty-first century. We will continue to promote interdisciplinary debate about ethnographic methods as the series grows. Most importantly, we will continue to champion ethnography as a valuable tool for apprehending a world in flux.

Alexander Thomas T. Smith
Department of Sociology, University of Warwick

Preface

The Boaz Trust night shelters offered emergency accommodation to refused and destitute male asylum seekers in Manchester, UK. Located in churches across the city, the network was established in 2008 and continued to operate until its closure in 2020 during the global COVID-19 pandemic. Although the network is no longer in operation, the needs it addressed have not gone away.

In its vicious complexity, the UK asylum system works to destabilise, marginalise and discourage people who have claimed protection under the 1951 Refugee Convention. Through a multi-pronged set of practices, including compulsory relocation, enforced destitution and indefinite detention, alongside an abiding culture of disbelief, it pushes many into a prolonged state of social and legal uncertainty without a means to support themselves or otherwise lead fulfilling lives. Detached from their official function as deterrents, these mechanisms can be more accurately described as forms of punishment for the very act of seeking sanctuary in the UK.

This book is a theoretically informed ethnography that draws on the stories and experiences of the men who used the Boaz Trust night shelters as well as the volunteers and employees who worked to support them. Although much of the research informing this book took place during a joint research project funded by the ESRC between the School of Geography, Queen Mary and the Centre for Cultural Studies, Goldsmiths between 2011 and 2016, it also extends before and beyond this time. The night shelters not only provided insight into the concrete effects of asylum policy on people and communities, but also serve as a prism for viewing the contemporary political landscape of the nation and the ubiquity of border regimes more widely as they shape both global life and the minutiae of the everyday.

Ethnography is a delicate craft in that it requires being attentive to people, places and things as they are formed and reformed by wider social, political and historic forces which are themselves ongoing and mutable. It is an embedded and situated practice that attempts to draw insight from both the mundane and the unique, the common and the singular. It works within fleeting moments and over extended periods of time. At its best, ethnography weaves together the granular and the panoramic, the personal and the social. Yet, just as words are written down the world seems to slip by and move on. It is here that the ethical impulse of ethnography is found. This book attempts to be both reflective and speculative. It turns to descriptions of life in the Boaz Trust night shelters at the same time that it strives to articulate a different order of things, however faint and hazy. It is an open call to break through the 'enchanted ordinary'[1] or the acceptance that things are as they are and cannot be otherwise. This is the restless justice that emerges from the stories and experiences of the men who lived in the Boaz Trust night shelters and the volunteers and employees who worked alongside them.

Note

1 This notion is borrowed from the critical race and legal theorist Vincent Lloyd. In his work on the late political philosopher Gillian Rose, Lloyd suggests that it is the task of philosophy to break through the enchanted ordinary or the soothing resignation that things are as they are and cannot be otherwise in favour of the 'translucent' ordinary which lays bare the uneven and unjust social stratifications of the world so as to transform them. (Lloyd, 2009: pp. 1–11).

Acknowledgements

Scholarship should never be considered an individual effort, particularly when it involves contributions from so many people and organisations. For this reason, I must express my deep gratitude to those who supported me while writing this book. This research was conducted with the Boaz Trust in Manchester and I would like to thank this incredible organisation not only for allowing me to work in the night shelters, but also for the support you provide to so many people across the city. In particular, I would like to thank Ros Holland, Sarah Beaney, Jonny Wilson, Vicky Ledwidge, Jean-Claude Kayumba, Katie Lifford and Vron Earp. I would also like to give a shout out to the Longsight Community Church and the people there. I would particularly like to thank Diego Lopez for his support. Both the Longsight Community Church and Boaz Trust are doing profound work in the city in the face of equally profound injustice. This research would not have been possible without the contributions of the night shelter volunteers and Boaz Trust employees. I also owe deep gratitude to those who were staying in the night shelters. Your hospitality, your encouragement, your criticisms and your willingness to share your insights and experiences are sincerely appreciated. I hope that, even in a small way, this research can provide an understanding of the consequences of our antagonistic immigration system with a view to transforming it.

This research was supported by the Economic and Social Research Council. I would also like to thank Marijke Hoek and the Seedbed Christian Community Trust for providing me with the space and time to extend this research and writing, and the Melbourne Social Equity Institute for the space they offered for writing. Prof. Jon May also provided close support, encouragement and challenging and inspiring advice throughout the process for which I am truly grateful. Prof. Nirmal Puwar, Dr. Camila Daniel and Amir Ghorbani took the time to read early drafts of my writing. Your feedback was invaluable. I also want to thank Prof. Jonathan Darling and Prof. Les Back for their careful review and insightful comments.

Les Back once said that we should take our writing for a walk. I perhaps took this too far. I lived in Manchester, London, Fukuoka, Melbourne and Galway while undertaking research and writing this book. I would like to thank all my friends in all these places for all the times you sat with me in a pub, izakaya or café and listened to me talk about this research, and for all the times that we didn't talk about it. I would also like to thank Manchester University Press for their guidance, encouragement and patience. I would also like to thank my parents, Rev. Dr. David Rainey and Alison Rainey. I would like to thank you for your care, concern, support and love always. I am your proud son. Finally, I would like to thank my amazing wife and companion, Prof. Tomoko Ichitani. Without you this research would not have started and it would not have finished. Your emotional, intellectual and economic support made it possible.

Abbreviations

ESRC	Economic and Social Research Council
FBO	faith-based organisation
IRC	Immigration Removal Centre
LCC	Longsight Community Church
NASS	National Asylum Support Service
NRPF	No Recourse to Public Funds
RESS	Restricted Eligibility Support Service
SMFC	South Manchester Family Church
UKBA	United Kingdom Border Agency

Introduction

At 8.30 pm on a cold Friday evening in mid-winter, a minibus pulls up outside the Longsight Community Church (LCC) in Manchester, UK. Twelve men step out and make their way into the building. They will be spending the night inside. The men are primarily from the Middle East, North Africa and sub-Saharan Africa and most have become destitute following the refusal of their asylum claim although others may have been granted refugee status and are experiencing a period of homelessness while they find employment and housing or access mainstream social services. In the UK, refused asylum seekers are denied the right to work and are placed under No Recourse to Public Funds (NRPF) which bars them from welfare support and public housing. They are also expected to leave the country although many are unwilling or unable to do so and subsequently live under threat of arrest, detention and deportation. Without a means to support themselves, many refused asylum seekers become dependent on charities to meet their most basic needs.

Inside the church a group of volunteers have prepared a hearty, warm meal and bedding and toiletries will be given out for the night. Some volunteers will join the meal before leaving while others will stay overnight, sleeping in the church alongside the men taking shelter. In the morning, after breakfast is prepared and shared, the sleeping bags, floor mats, blankets and supplies will be packed away and laundry gathered for collection. The church will be cleaned and locked, ready for the next community activity in an hour's time. The volunteers will make their way home or to work or wherever the day may take them while the men staying in the shelters will most likely make their way into central Manchester either by bus or on foot. Some might spend the day walking the streets or look for a place to keep warm such as a betting shop, a casino, a train station or the Arndale Shopping Centre. Some might see out the day in Manchester Central Library while others might visit friends or take up illicit and informal work, perhaps at a shisha cafe, at a food processing plant or delivering leaflets for a local takeaway. If they are Muslim, they might visit a local mosque and if it is Sunday and they are Christian, they might attend a church service. In the evening, the men will gather in the city centre to be picked up by a new set of volunteers and will be driven to another temporary shelter in another church for the night.

These scenes play out every day and night over the course of the winter months between November and April. The LCC is one of seven shelters operated by the Boaz Trust, a local faith-based organisation (FBO) that offers housing, emergency accommodation, legal support and advocacy to both female and male refused asylum seekers in the city. The night shelters are specifically available to men who would otherwise be sleeping rough and, although the Boaz Trust coordinates the shelter network, each church provides its own set of volunteers, food and supplies. Located throughout the city, from leafy middle-class suburbs to post-industrial working-class areas, the shelters are at once sites of displacement, on the fringes of public life and society while also being focal points of community activity formed in response to the injustices of the UK asylum system.

Stripped of their most basic rights, the men staying in the shelters are simultaneously abandoned by the UK Government and caught up in its bureaucratic processes as they try to re-engage with the asylum system by making a fresh claim, lodging an appeal or applying for forms of temporary state support. The men might stay in the shelters for days, weeks, months or over multiple winter seasons depending on their circumstances and opportunities. Some might move into housing provided by the Boaz Trust and live with other refused asylum seekers supported by the charity or move into hosted accommodation that the Boaz Trust arranges with local residents. Some might find accommodation through friends or personal networks while others might be offered temporary accommodation by the state on agreement that they leave the UK as soon as they are able to do so. Others might simply return to the street at the end of a winter season.

The night shelters are spaces of constant arrival and departure with around seventy different men from over twenty nationalities accessing the network at different points over a winter season (Boaz Trust, 2013: p. 9; Boaz Trust, 2018: p. 3; Longsight Community Church, 2016). Across the network around 300 volunteers (Boaz Trust, 2020: p. 5) from all walks of life and backgrounds prepare food, drive vehicles, wash bedding, replenish supplies, stay overnight and set up and take down the shelters. Working week-by-week or whenever they are scheduled and available, the volunteers keep the seven shelters running throughout the winter.

This book is partisan in its political and ethical engagement with the cruelty of the UK asylum system and border regimes more widely. It offers an 'ethnography of borders' to use Shahram Khosravi's phrase (Khosravi, 2011: p. 5). Based on research volunteering, managing and living in the shelters at different points between 2009 and 2018 as well as spending time around the city with the men using them, it draws on the stories, experiences and routines of refused asylum seekers to illuminate how abstract concepts of law and policy translate into the everyday life of those who have sought protection in the UK only to have their claims rejected. Such 'border stories' provide insight into the ongoing tragedy of the nation's asylum system and the chronic legal and social uncertainty it produces. Lives are put on hold as the system traps people in an 'eternal present' (Anderson, Sharma and Wright, 2009: p. 6) of prolonged waiting and anxious expectation. Days, weeks, months and even years unfold without the right to work or reside in the UK. Bound in this 'temporal straightjacket' (Back and Sinha, 2018: p. 7), people are unable to lead fulfilling lives or imagine a future.

For the men staying in the shelters the grinding boredom of repetitive days spent waiting for the next venue to open is superimposed by the antagonistic, dysfunctional and potentially threatening bureaucracy of the UK Home Office. This bifurcated waiting is punctuated by moments of frantic change as institutional processes speed up and slow down. A person might be required to move location at short notice once a fresh asylum claim has been made or a successful application for temporary state support has been granted or they may be subject to arrest, detention and deportation. These 'multiple temporal tensions' (Griffiths, 2014: p. 1991) and different velocities of waiting constitute a 'weaponised time' (Rainey, 2019a;

cf. Power, 2014) in which the state uses time to marginalise, delegitimise and exert control over individuals. This weaponised time sits alongside detention, destitution and the threat of deportation as a form of punishment for the very act of seeking protection in the UK.

This book also tracks the story of the Boaz Trust from its establishment in 2004 in response to growing numbers of refused asylum seekers accessing homeless support services in Manchester, through to the opening of the night shelter network in 2008 and its closure during the global COVID-19 pandemic. It details how the shelters simultaneously push against the malice of the UK asylum system by offering non-judgemental support to those who have been rejected while also being caught in the social stratification of bordering processes more broadly as fundamental differences between host and guest persist. The night shelters are spaces where 'mobile solidarities' (Squire, 2011) between precarious migrants and more established residents both form and fade. Moments of dignity and indignity, respect and shame emerge within everyday shelter life. For the men staying in the shelters, they are spaces of welcome, refuge and sociality. Yet, they are also spaces of restriction, restlessness and anxiety.

The Boaz Trust is a Christian organisation and takes its name from the Book of Ruth in the Old Testament where the figure of Boaz offers welcome and acceptance to Ruth who is a stranger in the land (Boaz Trust, 2025). Yet, across the shelter network both people of faith and no-faith work in support of those facing homelessness due to their immigration status. There has been increasing recognition that many FBOs are eschewing traditional 'salvationist' approaches to charitable work in which service provision is used as a vehicle for converting others, in favour of viewing charity as a form of social action seeking transformative change in the here and now (Beaumont and Baker, 2011; Beaumont and Cloke, 2012; Williams, Cloke and Thomas, 2012; Cloke, May and Johnsen, 2013; Cloke, Beaumont and Williams, 2013; Williams, 2015). Paul Cloke has introduced the term 'theo-ethics' to describe the ways in which religious faith can translate into practices of care towards others both organisationally and individually (Cloke, 2009; Cloke, 2010; Cloke, 2011). Informed by politicised theological concepts like love and justice which, as bell hooks reminds us (hooks, 2001: pp. 19,

30), are always intertwined, the theo-ethical crosses the sacred and the secular, the spiritual and the material.

The Boaz Trust and its employees and volunteers not only undertake the concrete work of service provision, but also pursue a prophetic counter-narrative to the disrespect, disbelief and inhumanity of the UK's asylum regime. The Boaz Trust describes this faith-motivated action as being 'restless for justice' in which 'we shine a light on injustice' and 'will fight to see change happen' (Boaz Trust, 2025). In the night shelters this restless justice was most often put into practice through mundane activities such as hoovering a church floor, preparing and sharing a meal, updating a volunteer rota or washing laundry. The Boaz Trust and the churches across the network were continually reworking, revising and adapting their practices and routines to improve their service amid changing circumstances and despite limited resources. Restless justice is the prosaic and banal infused with an imagination and desire to see the world otherwise. Yet this restless justice is also fragile and incomplete. It gains meaning through different and conflicting experiences and carries the possibility of missteps and mistakes as well as holding the potential to enact transformative change.

Spaces of asylum

Just after 7.00 am a volunteer switches on the lights at the Longsight Community Church. The main hall brightens up. Men are spread across the room lying on floor mats and tucked under blankets and sleeping bags. Bleary-eyed and with aching bodies after another night spent on another church floor, they begin to wake up. The smell of toast hangs in the air as volunteers make breakfast. Tea, coffee, eggs, fruit and cereal will also be laid out on a table in a room next to the hall. Some men make their way to the toilets and the shower while others begin to pack up their belongings. Others wrap themselves tighter in their blankets hoping to catch a bit more sleep. A volunteer will need to wake them up soon.

Over breakfast the men chat with each other and the volunteers. Conversations take place in multiple languages as Arabic, English, Farsi, French and Kurdish fill the room. Last night members of a local Korean church prepared the evening meal and people are still talking about how delicious it was. Some volunteers were born and raised in Manchester while others are migrants to the city. One volunteer is a postgraduate student from Trinidad studying biology at the University of Manchester while another stayed in the shelters a few years earlier and has returned to help after finding more stable accommodation. He has shared experiences with the men that other volunteers do not have.

Today a member of the church has made lunch bags for the men and after breakfast they inspect them and take them. There are sandwiches, crisps, chocolate bars and bottles of water. After packing away their sleeping bags and pillows and leaving their bedding in a pile to be picked up later by a volunteer doing laundry, the men make their way to Longsight and then to Manchester city centre. On a Saturday morning it's a forty-minute walk or fifteen-minute bus ride along Stockport Road. By 8.30 am the building is empty and locked. At 9.00 am the leaders from a Latin American church will arrive for their morning meeting in preparation for a church service in the building later that day.

We live in a world of 'divided connectedness' (Back and Sinha, 2018: p. 2), whether it is citizens, long-term residents and refused asylum seekers sharing breakfast with each other before going their separate ways, men making phone calls through Viber, WhatsApp and Skype to friends and family across the world from within a church hall in Longsight or the same men spending each day idle and restless in Manchester as they wait for the next shelter to open. It is a world where national border regimes have become a ubiquitous part of our day-to-day life and communities.

Borders are not simply lines on a map, nor are they only tied to specific sites such as a boundary wall or passport control. Rather, they are a set of regulations, practices, policies and laws that extend both spatially and temporally through society and operate unevenly across race, class and nationality (Balibar, 2002; Anderson, Sharma and Wright, 2009: pp. 6–7; Mezzadra and Neilson, 2012; Mezzadra and Neilson, 2013; Rainey, 2018; Rainey, 2019a: Walia, 2013: p. 37) They not only work to regulate flows of people in and out of a territory, but also produce different social and legal statuses within a territory. Borders continually shape and reshape people along a spectrum of highly racialised and classed subject positions – from the citizen to the diplomat and from the tourist to the refused asylum seeker – each with their own set of rights, restrictions and degrees of exposure to border enforcement. Although these processes may render distinctions between inside and outside ambiguous, the force and power of borders are retained. Freedoms, rights and mobilities are granted to some and denied to others. For some borders are inconsequential while for others they are an ever-present part of life whether though visa applications and continual engagement with bureaucratic systems or through the threat of deportation and detention.

Back at the breakfast table at the Longsight Community Church the international student volunteer undergoes continual attendance and visa checks at her university and her potential employment will be restricted to twenty hours a week during term time. Beside her, one of the men staying in the shelters expresses his fear of arrest during an upcoming meeting with immigration authorities. Yet, another volunteer, one who is a UK citizen, has little to no engagement with the border regime. The term 'differential inclusion' (Squire, 2009: p. 167; Mezzadra and Neilson, 2012; Mezzadra and Neilson, 2013: p. 159; Rainey, 2018) offers another way of describing this fractured sociality. It not only points to the ways in which borders multiply and stratify legal statuses among people within the same social space, but also how migrants are viewed as a constitutive outside, temporarily incorporated into the territorial order as a threatening supplement, in order to bolster notions of national belonging and sovereignty. In other words, migrants are included in the sovereign order through their very exclusion. This is what Giorgio Agamben refers to as the 'ban' as a person is placed outside recourse to the law while remaining subject to its intervention and violence (1998).

The Boaz Trust night shelters, with an array of people across different social and legal statuses, are a microcosm of differential inclusion. They are what I term 'spaces of asylum'. Spaces of asylum are where the legal and social processes of asylum policy are played out. This definition is intentionally broad as it allows for the deep contradictions between refuge and abandonment that are contained within the word 'asylum' to come to the fore. Spaces of asylum are spaces in which borders are enacted, bringing together an often conflicting set of notions such as inclusion and exclusion, movement and fixity, practices of care and resistance alongside forms of containment, control and incarceration. They are spaces where the multiple and discordant temporalities that emerge when an individual is maintained in a temporary status – whether as refused asylum seeker or asylum seeker – pan out over the long term. In this respect they do not rely on a singular or narrowly defined border, but instead how law, policy and practice are enacted across multiple sites and multiple scales as the border is borne in the social-legal status of individuals, both within and beyond the formal boundaries of the nation state. These spaces can include ports, pre-entry interceptions on sea or land, off-shore detention centres and inland detention centres, or state-sponsored housing offered to people while their claims are processed. While some of these examples are more inhumane than others, they all serve to restrict what Vicki Squire refers to as the political space of asylum (Squire, 2009: p. 116). In this political sense, spaces of asylum are spaces of refuge and sanctuary, as well as individual and collective potential. This is at odds with the more adversarial examples above and the concept ultimately emerges dialectically, brimming with contradiction as conflicting values, discourses and practices shift within it. The streets of Manchester are spaces of asylum as well as the night shelters. So too are train stations, detention centres, bookmakers and libraries. In this respect the concept 'spaces of asylum' can challenge certain framings of migrants while at the same time recognising that statist rationalities remain prevalent. It is such tensions that inform my account of the Boaz Trust night shelters.

As spaces of asylum the night shelters are located on the edge of what Bridget Anderson has termed the 'community of value' (2013). Anderson writes that modern nation states increasingly portray themselves as a 'community of value' in which certain people matter more than others – and belong more than others – because they are imagined to act in good and proper ways and fit within the norms of social and family life (Anderson, 2013: pp. 2–5; Jones *et al.*, 2017: pp. 121–2). The community of value is heavily racialised and classed and the 'good citizen' who is regarded as a hard-working and law-abiding member of a stable and respectable family, is contrasted with the benefits claimant and the migrant. The benefits claimant can easily be imagined as the 'benefits scrounger' and the migrant can easily be imagined as 'illegal' and therefore criminal. The easy conflation of migrant and 'illegal migrant' in public and political discourse seeps into our understanding of 'asylum seeker' or 'refugee' and the bearers of these labels can then conveniently be configured as culpable outsiders who have entered the country without permission and refused to leave, an affront to the nation's attempt to control its borders and therefore an affront to its very sovereignty. The community of value is grounded in a set of deserving and underserving distinctions, such as the good immigrant and 'illegal immigrant' or the genuine and 'bogus' asylum seeker, that radiate from the centre outwards, shaping contemporary social and political life both practically and discursively. Operating at the edge of the community of value, the night shelters were spaces where communities formed responses to the crisis of policy-produced destitution on the city's streets by putting into practice a prophetic radicalism through acts of care and love, offering a counter-narrative to the current order.

On the surface, borders appear simple. Yet, on a deeper level they are socially, materially and legally complex. A key concluding insight I wish to make here is that, in their simultaneous intricacy and taken-for-grantedness, borders can be grasped as a form of 'concrete abstraction'. This is a notion taken from Henri Lefebvre that describes the ill-fitting relationship between reified concepts and everyday social life (Lefebvre, 1991; Stanek, 2008; Stanek, 2011; Gromark, 2013; Hanson and Rainey, 2020). It articulates the gap between the oversimplified categories we use to make sense of the world and the complex ways in which social life is actually produced. It is in this sense that national borders take on the contradictory quality of being at once abstract and concrete. In political discourse and the public imagination, borders have become detached from the historical, ideological and social conditions that produce and maintain them. Instead, they are fetishised as ideal objects, as sheer lines of distinction between inside and outside. Understood to be fixed and natural, a particular border is taken as something that needs to be defended, protected and controlled. It holds symbolic power as a marker for national sovereignty, authority and integrity which then translates into policy and practice in our everyday world. In other words, the abstract can easily bear down on the concrete and borders take on a malign force that extends both spatially and temporally across social life, setting the contours of differential inclusion and the community of value. It is a task of the ethnographer to remove the gloss of this concrete abstraction and render it translucent, bringing to light the vicious complexity of border regimes and the ways in which they shape lives in often divisive and troubling ways. It is through vivid descriptions of everyday life under the asylum system that the possibility of considering the world differently emerges.

Outline of the book

Ethnography is both reflective and speculative. It is a diagnostic practice that also gives expression to emergent political and social possibilities within everyday life. Through the border stories and experiences of the men staying in the Boaz Trust night shelters and the people working to support them, this book aims to give articulation to the restless justice that is practiced in spaces and communities in Manchester. In doing so, this book has three main objectives. The first is to offer a description of lives being lived under the 'slow violence' (Darling, 2023) of the UK's border regime, where individuals are left in a prolonged state of social and legal uncertainty, facing destitution and unable to imagine a future. It sheds light on a crisis being faced by those who have had their claims for protection refused and whose stories are often overlooked amid the wider, often vitriolic, political and public discourse surrounding asylum and immigration. Secondly, in its account of the night shelters, it indicates how resistance to the cruelty of national asylum policy is being undertaken at a local level through the work of FBOs, communities and individuals. In this respect, the Boaz Trust and the churches operating emergency night shelters are not merely service providers but organisations and people offering prophetic counter-narratives to the inhumanity of the asylum regime, putting into practice a restless justice through everyday acts of organisation and care. Finally, it sets these accounts within a wider understanding of borders as being contradictory entities, at once abstract and diffuse, ideological and material, simple and complex. With their symbolic power as markers of national sovereignty and integrity, they hold sway in our social life, through regulations, practices, policies and laws that divide and stratify, shaping lives in often malign ways as the abstract bears down on the concrete.

Chapter 1 begins on the streets of Manchester as the men staying in the night shelters see out each day waiting for the next venue to open for the night. Hours are spent idle and restless. It is an emotionally charged time filled with anxiety and boredom. It is a time shaped by a doubled placelessness as the men not only have nowhere to call home, but their very presence in the country is called into question. Time on the street is a weaponised time that takes the form of a bifurcated waiting in which the mundane and repetitive experience of seeing out each day from a position of destitution is superimposed by the vicious, prolonged and often dysfunctional processes of the asylum system. Yet, the street is also where people 'get by' and places such as Manchester Central Library, coach stations and bookmakers are made and remade as 'spaces of asylum' which are inscribed with a number of dialectical tensions across refuge and abandonment, dignity and indignity, hostility and care. It is such tensions that characterise life on the streets for destitute and refused asylum seekers.

Chapter 2 is a methodological chapter that reflects on the policy landscape of the UK in relation to ethnographic research alongside people who have been refused asylum. Identifying dispersal, destitution, denial and weaponised time as the four key pillars of the UK asylum system, it suggests that these function less as forms of deterrence and more as forms of punishment for the very act of seeking sanctuary in the UK. The chapter begins by exploring the revelatory power of emotions in such a context as they become a lens to not only understand the fragile dynamics of participant observation but also the wider social and political landscape of contemporary Britain. Emotions cut across the political and the personal and confound the formal categories of ethnographic work including 'researcher' and 'field'. It offers a reflection on my own experience as a migrant to the UK as well as my changing approach to the Christian faith in a research context shaped by religious organisations and practice. It also outlines how this research project took shape as a form of 'extended place method' (Duneier, 1999) where initial work volunteering in one of the Boaz Trust night shelters would extend to the entire shelter network as well as ethnographic work on the streets and other spaces of the city.

Chapter 3 tracks the history of the Boaz Trust and the night shelters within the changing policy landscape of the UK. Founded in 2004 amid the introduction and implementation of increasingly restrictive and exclusionary asylum legislation, the Boaz Trust has grown from providing a few spare rooms in Manchester to being a major service organisation in the city offering housing, advocacy, legal and financial support and a range of well-being activities to people accessing its services. With its basis in Christian practice, the Boaz Trust is a faith-based organisation that adopts a holistic and person-centred approach to service provision that eschews traditional salvationist models of charity, with their emphasis on conversion and evangelism, in favour of being 'restless for justice' and seeing social change and the outworking of the Kingdom of God in the here and now. This restless justice carries eschatological weight is it counters an unjust asylum system with a practical, if localised, alternative vision based on dignity and welcome.

Chapter 4 turns to the work of the volunteers within the night shelters with a particular focus on the Longsight Community Church. It indicates how the churches in the shelter network functioned as community centres as much as places of formal worship and suggests that restless justice was often put into practice through mundane day-to-day activities such as preparing and sharing meals, driving transport to and from the shelters, setting up and putting away shelter supplies and cleaning and preparing venues, among other things. Christian love or *agape* emerged as a core value for many volunteers while volunteers also recognised the limitations of shelter work, suggesting that, ultimately, restless justice is an often fragile and incomplete task.

Chapter 5 returns to the night shelters but from the perspective of the men staying in them. It describes how the night shelters were spaces of transition without resolution in the ongoing lives of those living with uncertain legal and social statuses. It uses the appellatives of the 'waiting room' and 'locked room', which are drawn from the men using the spaces, to describe not only the night shelters but also the wider restrictive asylum policies and border practices of the UK that gave rise to them. The night shelters were restless spaces of constant relocation and sleeplessness as well as provisional spaces where up to one hundred men continually arrived and departed over the course of a winter season. While providing a transition from the street, with opportunities for safety and sociality, they were also spaces dominated by the weaponised time of the UK asylum system. As such the night shelters remained 'spaces of asylum' with all the dialectical tension between care and disturbance, welcome and abandonment that this term entails.

Although the Boaz Trust night shelters permanently closed following the global COVID-19 pandemic, the conditions which gave rise to them have not gone away. In their wake new forms of service provision have emerged through which the Boaz Trust continues frontline work for those facing destitution on account of their immigration status. The conclusion returns to the continuing border stories of men who passed through the shelters, but there is little closure or heartwarming resolution to offer. Instead we continue to see how the border regime can leave people in a prolonged social and legal uncertainty where lives are cut short and futures foreclosed. It is in these conditions that a restless justice emerges that is put into practice through everyday acts of care and solidarity, that are infused with a desire to see the world otherwise.

1

Time on the street

On a bitterly cold Sunday morning in early December a minibus pulls up alongside Piccadilly Gardens in central Manchester. Twelve men who have just spent the night in a Boaz Trust night shelter step out onto the pavement. Some will immediately head into the city while others hang around the street, deciding what to do for the day. As it is a Sunday, the city streets are nearly deserted and there is none of the usual bustle of a weekday morning. It also means that many of the public buildings the men regularly frequent during the day will be closed. Alternative spaces to keep warm and see out the hours will need to be found. Arriving in central Manchester after a night spent sleeping on a church floor is a daily experience for the men. It is a moment that not only takes place on any given Sunday, but also throughout the week over the course of a winter season.

Time on the street is a part of everyday shelter life. It is the repetitive and mundane experience of seeing out each day, waiting for the shelters to open and close, without the right to work and without a place to call one's own. Days unfold from a position of privation and are accompanied by an underlying uncertainty over one's legal status and future. Under UK policy, asylum seekers are denied the right to work and refused asylum seekers are placed under No Recourse to Public Funds (NRPF) which bars access to mainstream welfare support and public housing. Refused asylum seekers are also expected to leave the country, though many are unwilling or unable to do so. It is an enforced destitution that becomes an enforced waiting and idleness. Time on the street is a policy-produced form of 'chronic waiting' founded on the exclusion of refused asylum seekers, who are deemed unwanted and superfluous and placed outside legal and, therefore, social norms (Jeffrey,

2008: pp. 954–5). A logic of differential inclusion is at work in shaping time on the street and the everyday lives of the men staying in the Boaz Trust night shelters, both young and old, who have been rejected by the British state. Suspicions concerning the genuineness of their asylum claims call into question their honesty and integrity and ultimately begin to strip away their dignity as they face repetitive, hollowed out days waiting for the next shelter to open. Time on the street is an emotionally loaded time filled with feelings of emptiness, anxiety, boredom, isolation, indignity and loneliness. Yet, the rejection of their asylum claims and consequent wasted time and emotional degradation is instrumental in shoring up what Bridget Anderson terms 'the community of value' with its need to exclude people – morally, socially and legally – in order to consolidate a cohesive sense of British national identity and common moral worth, while also validating official claims that immigration is being brought under control.

Research alongside asylum seekers has often focused on 'events' within their lives such as the journey, detention or asylum interview rather than the everyday life of waiting between these events. Perhaps, as Rebecca Rotter suggests, this is because it is assumed that nothing of importance or interest happens in these between times (Rotter, 2015). This chapter gives account of this everyday life of waiting as the men using the Boaz Trust night shelters pass their time on the streets. This is a time not only shaped by the constraining rhythms of a dysfunctional bureaucracy but also impelled by meeting basic needs such as keeping warm, staying safe and combatting boredom. It is the experience of a weaponised time in the form of a bifurcated waiting, both mundane and anxious as hours and days spent idle are superimposed by an antagonistic and potentially threatening border regime.

Writing about time on the street has its difficulties as it must not only convey the experience of extended periods of idleness, but also apprehend its heavy emotional weight, laden with feelings of uncertainty, fear and shame. In late 2013, Victor brought a pile of documents to the Sunday night shelter in Ashton-Under-Lyne. They related to his asylum case and he had been storing them at his friend's house, along with some other personal possessions, while he stayed in the shelters. Victor had spent three nights sleeping rough in central Manchester following weeks couch-surfing at a friend's place after being released from Harmondsworth Immigration Removal Centre (IRC). He was in his mid-thirties and originally from Cameroon although had lived in Nigeria for many years before making his way to the UK. His life between these three countries had been shaped by conflict, violence and imprisonment. Victor had claimed asylum after being arrested in a bus station in London for overstaying his Visitor's Visa, a claim that was swiftly rejected while in detention. The thick bundle of papers he brought to the shelter was a growing archive of his time in the UK including arrest reports, police statements, asylum interview transcripts, court judgments, appeals forms, letters of rejection, a release form from Harmondsworth IRC and documents he had been collecting, including newspaper clippings, for a possible fresh asylum claim.

The next morning, he passed the documents on to me as we sat together in Manchester Central Library. Victor wasn't seeking my advice, but was doing so, he said, in order that I could better understand his situation. They were a comprehensive account of his asylum claims process. I read through each document, one by one, before handing them back to Victor. We agreed to record an interview that day and later we made the short walk to the Royal Exchange Theatre and spoke in the open, but quiet and private space of the atrium. We discussed a lot of things – his encounter with immigration authorities following his arrest, his experiences in detention, the processing of his asylum claim, his thoughts on the night shelters and his hopes and dreams for the future. We also talked about his weeks spent couch-surfing and his days sleeping rough in central Manchester which formed a sort of 'between time' that was not covered by any official documentation or charitable engagement.

I asked Victor about his experiences on the street and he spoke of dizziness, loneliness and how he struggled to hold back the tears. He then became hesitant while speaking, giving short, emotive answers before finally saying, 'I felt very lonely, but I don't want to go back there'. This comment doesn't come across well on paper. Victor wasn't talking about a possible return to sleeping rough at some point in the future. By not wanting to 'go back there' he meant not wanting to recall the experience during our interview. Amid all the papers documenting his experiences of violence in Cameroon and Nigeria and his reasons for seeking asylum, as well as our discussion on detention centres, the night shelters and the asylum claims process, it was living on the street that Victor found to be the most difficult thing to speak about at that moment. He normally carried himself with a friendly and quiet poise and constantly prodded me with questions, insights and critical comments on my research but in asking him about his time on the street – his experience of homelessness – I seemed to be stripping back a sense of pride and dignity. We quickly moved the discussion on.

Salah also arrived in the night shelters in early 2013. He was a former engineering student from Cairo who had claimed asylum while studying at a university in London and had been living in state-backed but privately operated National Asylum Support Service (NASS) accommodation in Manchester while his claim was processed and eventually rejected. With no place to go and fearing a return to Egypt, Salah faced the prospect of sleeping rough and so he approached the accommodation management with a code of conduct form he had been given while receiving NASS support. It included the threat that any breaches of the code could lead to detention in an IRC. Salah pointed out all the times he had broken the rules and volunteered himself for detention. It was a desperate attempt to avoid becoming street homeless. Nothing came of this and he had presented himself to a refugee support agency in Manchester who referred him to the Boaz Trust night shelters. Time on the street is a deeply troubling and emotive landscape. Victor's comments and eventual withdrawal from the topic during the interview and Salah's attempt to be detained are indicative of this in their own ways. They are also indicative of the fear, isolation and shame that can hang over those rendered destitute by the UK's asylum system.

Doubled placelessness

Drawing on the work of the American homeless rights activist Mitch Snyder, Samira Kawash writes that a central issue of the experience of homelessness is 'how to pass time without any space' (Snyder and Hombs, 1982: p. 110; Kawash, 1998: p. 328). This is a problem encountered under the 'condition of placelessness' (Kawash, 1998: p. 329). Placelessness, for Kawash, is the experience of dispossession and a contraction of social existence and possibility. It is having no place to be. It is being without a place to call one's own. It is not having a place to rest, be safe or leave one's things. The concept describes how people experiencing homelessness are rendered 'out of place' in the words of Talmadge Wright (1997), pushed to the edge of the community of value as failed citizens or 'illegal' immigrants in the public imagination. In the case of the men staying in the Boaz Trust night shelters, this 'placelessness' was a direct result of asylum policy (see the following chapter) which casts individuals as limited figures in relation to the public (cf. Kawash, 1998: p. 129).

As Jones *et al.* write, migrants are not allowed to be 'ordinary' in the public imagination. Rather, they must be extraordinary – rendered as culpable or helpless, 'genuine' or 'abusive' (Jones *et al.*, 2017: pp. 365–6). Such tropes diminish the complex experiences and capacities of people seeking asylum (see Boochani, 2018: pp. 364–6). In his autobiographical work *'Illegal' Traveller* Shahram Khosravi describes how there is a particular image of the 'refugee' that holds sway in public discourse.

> [...] Pain and suffering have become the hallmarks of refugeeness. The term 'refugee' generally signifies deprived and underprivileged people. A 'real' refugee is thus supposed to be a 'profound', 'poor', 'traumatized', 'serious' and of course 'sad' person (Khosravi, 2011: p. 73).

As such the image of the refugee is a concrete abstraction, deployed in relation to a wider, normative, but also imagined national community. It is an image conjured to affirm the legitimacy and hospitality of the host nation, while also reducing the agency of individuals by moralising on their status, behaviour and appearance. It is an image that masks a complex reality.

Many of the men staying in the Boaz Trust night shelters were casually or smartly dressed and bore no relation to the visual markers of the imagined 'homeless body' or suffering refugee. 'A happy, well-dressed, good-looking refugee is a contradiction', writes Khosravi (2011). Yet, the men in the Boaz Trust night shelters remained in the 'condition of placelessness', without a space to call one's own, without a home. They remained homeless in the sense that it is used to describe individuals who are sleeping rough or otherwise lack settled accommodation and this includes people in temporary or insecure forms of accommodation, such as night shelters (Johnsen, Cloke and May, 2008: p. 205). But, this is also a doubled placelessness, as they exist in a state of 'irregularity' where the norms and rules taken for granted by all citizens cease to apply and everyday activities or possibilities such as working, travelling, accessing education, housing and healthcare may be criminalised or severely restricted (Khosravi, 2011: p. 90). It is in this sense that the men staying in the Boaz Trust night shelters faced a condition of 'doubled placelessness' – it is the placelessness of being without stable accommodation as well as the placelessness of a refused asy-lum seeker who is without the right to work, access public funds and remain in the UK. Their very presence within the bounds of the nation state is called into question. This doubled placelessness binds individuals to a perpetual state of movement as they 'are forced into constant motion not because they are going somewhere, but because they have nowhere to go. Going nowhere is simultaneously being nowhere; homelessness is not only being without home, but more generally without place' (Kawash, 1998: p. 327). In this way the condition of placelessness, and doubled placelessness, returns to the dilemma posed earlier – of how to pass time without any space. Time on the street is the working through of this dilemma, with its continual oscillation between movement and idleness, walking and waiting and managing destitution by finding small ways to 'get by' on a day-to-day basis while also engaging with an abstruse and punitive asylum system.

Walking and waiting

I wish to return to that Sunday morning in early December in Piccadilly Gardens, as the day opened out to the men staying in the night shelters. Although most of the men departing the minibus quickly made their way into the city, three remained standing on the pavement at the edge of the square. The small group was still unsure about what to do for the day. It was Wasim, a well-built and verbose man, originally from the Gaza Strip, who invited me to join them. Alongside him were Hani and Naveed. Hani was also from Palestine and closely accompanied Wasim during their time in the night shelters. He was shy and withdrawn and spoke little English and remained quiet around other Arabic speakers. He wore an awkward purple hat with a wide, circular brim. It looked almost comical and sometimes Wasim would remove it without warning and expose Hani's balding head. Whenever Wasim did this, others around would laugh and smile while Hani remained silent and expressionless. Naveed was in his mid-sixties and originally from Pakistan. He had spent years living precariously in the UK as an asylum seeker and then refused asylum seeker before arriving in the Boaz Trust night shelters where he would spend three months sleeping on different church floors. Naveed was talkative, sociable and attentive to others who were staying in the shelters. He often made cups of tea for people and ensured that others around him always had enough bedding for the night. I had become close to both Naveed and Wasim during my stay in the shelters and we shared many conversations over hot drinks, during meals and throughout the evenings as we prepared to sleep. We spent hours together walking the city streets and around the Arndale Shopping Centre or sitting in the foyer of the Boaz Trust offices, seeing out the day.

Although Wasim had a strong personality, often took the lead on the streets and could easily dominate the conversation in the shelters, it was Naveed who suggested that we make our way to a 'church' that provided space for homeless persons during the day. The church Naveed spoke of was the Beacon Drop-in Centre on Richmond Street, parallel to Canal Street, otherwise known as 'The Gay Village', an LGBTQ district in the city. Operated by Barnabus, a Christian charity, the Beacon Centre offers food, sanctuary, basic medical care, hot showers and other services to people experiencing homelessness in the city. However, it is only open five days a week and was closed that Sunday. In the biting cold of that December morning we retraced our steps back towards Piccadilly Gardens, stopping at the Chorlton Street Coach Station. It had seating and was warm. We would spend the next five hours there.

While Naveed was leading us to the Beacon Centre, Wasim had approached a man standing outside the coach station. Initially intending to ask him for a cigarette, Wasim quickly recognised him from other homeless services in the city and from the casinos they both frequented. He joined us as we walked to the Beacon Centre – also not realising that it was closed – and then returned to the coach station with us. He was reserved and quiet and spoke very little, although seemed happy with the company. While sitting in the waiting area of the coach station, I began a conversation with him. His name was Yevgeny and he said he was from Siberia but had lived in Munich for the past three years before arriving in Manchester. When I asked him if he had liked Munich he replied with sharp sarcasm, 'If I liked it, I wouldn't be in Manchester, would I?'. The conversation was short. He stayed with us for another three hours, sitting in silence, before suddenly taking a casino chip from his pocket and saying, 'this will get me into the casino. Maybe I'll win something'. This was the last I saw of him. Meeting Yevgeny in passing that early December morning, as he sat quietly in the coach station for so many hours before walking off, would prefigure the transience I would encounter in the night shelters as people suddenly left and moved on, arriving with little notice and departing without further contact.

Gerald Daly writes that 'for people without housing, who live on the streets, their days are marked by endless walking and waiting' (1996: p. 128). That Sunday in early December, like other days, would involve prolonged periods of walking and waiting, movement and stasis, with little immediate purpose beyond seeing out the day until the next shelter opened. That day began with a walk through the city centre, following Naveed, and would then include walking to Manchester Aquatics Centre – near Manchester Metropolitan University – and back, as well as passing through the casinos of Chinatown.

Waiting takes on particular meanings under the condition of doubled placelessness which, as I have argued, not only includes the condition of being without a home or place to call one's own, but also the condition of irregularity and legal uncertainty that, in the case of the refused asylum seeker, prohibits employment and access to public funds and which places one's very presence in the UK under constant question. 'Waiting is an urgent matter', writes Jean-François Bayart and it is a particularly urgent matter for those caught up in the regulatory regimes of international migration and who are rendered superfluous and unwanted by the state (Bayart, 2007: pp. 269, 272). For Bayart, waiting is a symptom of being in a state of 'permanent displacement' (p. 282). It is waiting shaped by the politics of abandonment, as the law withdraws its support at the same time that it maintains its authority, pushing individuals on a slide towards 'bare life' (Agamben, 1998) and into what Bayart terms a 'permanent state of stand-by' (Bayart, 2007: p. 272). It is waiting shaped by differential inclusion as individuals are 'forced into latency' – present yet not visible – not only in segregated sites like detention centres, but also, as I am suggesting, on the city streets and in the heart of civic space (p. 269).

Walking was a means of passing time. It was a form of waiting. Early one Friday morning I joined Wasim, Naveed, Hani and two others as they left the shelter in Broughton, Salford. It was some distance from Manchester city centre, yet like others leaving the shelters that morning they decided to walk into the city centre despite being given bus fare by the church operating the night shelter. Walking also became a means of saving money and some of the group pooled their bus fares together to buy a packet of cigarettes to share. Wasim would also tell me how important it was to save money in order to top up on mobile phone credit in order to keep in touch with family back home. I spent most of that walk with Naveed, who was a non-smoker. He planned to spend the £3 he had been given in a pound shop and purchase earphones so he could listen to the radio, as well as some biscuits and water. It was an hour and a half walk to the city centre, over five kilometres, and from there to the Boaz Trust offices where we would spend the day in their communal area, warm.

Walking had its purposes beyond saving money. Naveed spoke of its health benefits saying, 'it's good to be active and walking is healthy'. As if to further justify the need to walk such long distances, he also added that walking allowed you to see the city. Wasim overhead this last comment and began to laugh, pointing to the Salford skyline saying, 'but what is there to look at?'. In other conversations Naveed described how walking formed part of his daily routine as he would spend the day 'walking around Piccadilly' in the city centre, unless the weather was poor in which case he would spend the day in Manchester Central Library – at the time temporarily located on Deansgate as the main building near the Town Hall underwent a three-year refurbishment. Others adopted similar routines and during that same winter season I would often see Babir, a young Kurdish man originally from Iraq, walking around the Arndale Shopping Centre as he waited for the shelters to open.

It was a safe, warm and public environment where he could blend in with and observe the crowds of shoppers.

One evening, as we waited on the street for transport to the shelters, some of the men described their day to me. After leaving the shelter in Didsbury, south Manchester, they had walked to the Rainbow Haven day centre in Openshaw, east Manchester. From there they had walked to the Boaz Trust offices in Ancoats, covering a total of eleven kilometres over the course of the day.

The street was not only a place for walking to pass time, save money, or keep active, but also for fostering interaction and opportunities with other members of the public. This was particularly the case for Wasim, whose effusive and outgoing personality would see him approach strangers for cigarettes, say 'good morning' to passers-by and, more awkwardly for us around him, wolf whistle and cat call to women we passed on the street. While these actions shifted between the friendly and the crude, they were also strategic. Wasim described to me his technique for obtaining cigarettes which was carefully planned so as to avoid the appearance of begging. He would greet a person and then ask, 'Do you smoke?'. If they replied 'yes', he would ask, 'What's your favourite brand?' while simultaneously ruffling his hand in his pocket – an action suggesting that Wasim was about to pull out his own cigarettes and display his favourite brand. Yet, his question would often lead to the stranger pulling out their own cigarettes to show Wasim. At this point he would pull a lighter from his pocket, rather than cigarettes, and ask the stranger for one of theirs and then light them both. In this respect, there was a certain degree of 'blagging' to these interactions and Wasim would later tell me, with pride, that he had the skill of 'convincing people that they want to give me something that I need'.

My last conversation with Wasim was on a Friday night in the Longsight Community Church shelter in late January 2013. It was the evening before a date he had arranged with a woman he had met on the street and Wasim asked my advice on whether he should wash his jacket so as to make a better impression. He was nervous and tense. The woman he had met only days earlier had been texting him throughout the day telling him what she expected and wanted from a new boyfriend. He felt under pressure, but it was also a way out of the shelters. This was the last time I would see

Wasim and rumour among other men staying in the shelters was that he had moved in with her.

While walking was described as a useful way of passing time, saving money, and keeping active, less positive descriptions also emerged. Wasim would sometimes talk about his life immediately prior to arriving in the shelter network. He spoke about wandering the streets of Manchester in a morose stupor. These recollections did not refer to any specific length of time but were rather descriptions of his state of mind and physical health during an intense period of depression over his destitution. Wasim described how he developed a limp to cope with the severe pain he began to feel in his feet, while at the same time ignoring the growing concerns of strangers who watched him pass by. His wandering lasted until his feet turned black and blue, apparently from gangrene. An eventual visit to the hospital, which should provide primary care to refused asylum seekers, led to an injection that eliminated the condition. 'I almost lost my feet, Mark', Wasim once said after recalling his time walking adrift and injured through the streets of the city.

The streets could be sites of indignity, isolation, and shame. They could also be sites where violence occasionally erupted. Wasim spoke about a man, originally from Pakistan, who owed him money. Wasim had confronted him multiple times, roughing him up on the streets of Rusholme or, on one occasion, dragging him by the ear from a betting shop. Each time Wasim would claim whatever cash the man had on him. Wasim preferred it that way rather than being paid back in a lump sum, as it meant he had a quick source of cash if needed. Naveed carried a business card with him on the streets. It had a contact number for the United Kingdom Border Agency (UKBA) (now the UK Border Force) and it was his option of last resort if a confrontation or argument ever escalated or became threatening. Naveed described how he would pull the card out from his pocket and threaten to call the immigration authorities, putting himself and any others at risk. For Naveed, this had been a useful way to diffuse any aggression and intimidation he had encountered on the streets.

In relation to street homelessness, Robert Desjarlais writes that 'the dominant chronotope of the street was one of drifting unmoored, with very few demarcated ends or places' (1997: p. 128). For the men living in the Boaz Trust shelters, time on the street could be both banal and anxious, filled with prolonged boredom and yet, also, potentially aggressive and violent moments. Walking the streets was often a 'drifting unmoored' – whether around the Arndale Shopping Centre, around Piccadilly Gardens, or on extended walks between shelters, service points, and the city centre. It was a means of 'passing time without any space'. Walking and waiting were the products of the temporality of 'doubled placelessness', an unyielding mixture of grinding boredom and poverty and repetitive days spent arriving and departing from different shelters, without a place of one's own and without the right to work, all superimposed by the antagonistic and potentially threatening bureaucratic processes of the UK asylum system.

Manchester Central Library and the bookmakers as spaces of asylum

The public entrance to Manchester Town Hall Extension is directly across from the Friends Meeting House on Mount Street, beside Albert Square in central Manchester. The entrance is set within a colonnade that runs along the outside of the large, neo-classical building. Inside, the visitor is met with a sweeping, curved hall with a lofty ceiling. A number of large sofas and chairs line the right-hand side. It is a grand space that leads on to both the City Council's Customer Service Centre and the Media Lounge which has a range of PC terminals, Mac terminals, and gaming stations for public use. On a wall linking the two areas is a sign reading: 'No matter who you are or where you are from, Manchester is, and always will be, yours'. It's a busy space. There are people queuing at counters to access housing support and other council services, and there are meetings between advisers and members of the public taking place at desks across the open-plan area, while others are sitting at, or moving between, terminals in the Media Lounge. Between 2013 and 2014 the area was even busier as the Media Lounge served as the temporary location for Manchester Central Library while the main building underwent its three-year refurbishment.

In late 2013 I spent hours, and days, in the temporary library with Victor and some of the other men who were staying in the shelters. Each morning we would walk across the city centre from the drop-off point, which was typically outside the Boaz Trust offices in Ancoats or alongside Piccadilly Gardens in the city centre, and make our way to the Town Hall Extension, through its curved entrance hall, and into the library space. This space was filled with mobile shelving units, tables, and a temporary library desk where visitors could be issued with library cards, return or take out books, and book times at the always-busy PC terminals.

Victor and I would normally take our seats at a large, round table that was prominently placed at the back of the temporary library. Despite arriving early each morning, we would often find that the table was already quite busy with others sitting around it, and other chairs and desks around the space were also already filling up. Sitting at the large table brought us together with other regular users of the library who would also spend their days there. Victor was a former schoolteacher and had often spoken of his plans to become a licenced accountant if he was ever given status to remain and work in the UK. Each morning he would take an accountancy textbook from the shelves, pull out a pen and a paper, and work through a chapter of exercises. He told me that it was a way of keeping his mind active during the relatively empty days while living in the shelters. On the first day we arrived in the library together, Victor signed up for a library card so that he could take out books and read them in the afternoon or take them to the shelters in the evening. A library card also allowed a person to book times at the PC terminals and Victor would use it as an opportunity to connect to the internet.

Others also joined us in the library. Adil, a young surgeon in his early thirties and originally from Sudan, sometimes spent time there studying for an English course he was taking in the hope of working in the National Health Service in the future. Adil had been granted refugee status in the UK but was going through a period of homelessness as he struggled to find work and housing. In early December 2013, Adil secured accommodation in a hostel and it was in the library that I would last see him. We hugged and wished each other luck, he with his future and I with my research.

Other men who had stayed in the shelters also described how important the library was as a place to spend the day. Salah and his friend Temir who was originally from Iraq spoke of how they would spend time together in the temporary library. Salah spoke about reading books on local history, while Temir described how he would sometimes ask the librarian for information on a specific topic in order to appear a student doing research in the library, rather than someone who was destitute and passing time there. Other libraries, beyond Manchester Central Library, were used too. Betin was a young Kurdish man from Iran who had arrived in the UK as a minor and had received temporary refugee status only to have his asylum claim rejected once he reapplied as an adult. While living in the night shelters in late 2014 and early 2015, Betin said he would sometimes return to Oldham, a northern borough of Greater Manchester, and spend the day in the local library where he had friends and knew the people working there. Similarly, Nasir, who stayed in the night shelters over the winter of 2017–18 would often spend his days in the Longsight Library in south Manchester where he could read books, connect to the internet or rest in the library's chairs. Prior to arriving in the night shelters, Nasir had spent time sleeping rough in a homeless camp in Longsight Market with a group of other people experiencing destitution and knew that part of the city well.

On occasion, during the hours we spent in the library, Victor and I would take turns sleeping at the table, as the nights spent on different church floors left us with aching bodies and near-constant tiredness. I once fell into a deep sleep only to be woken up by a private security guard shaking my shoulder as I lay folded over the table. He was employed by G4S, worked in the library and would periodically wake people up who had fallen asleep. 'Are you alright?', he asked. It took me a while to compose myself after being woken up from my slumber. I nodded, bleary-eyed, and after the security guard had left Victor started laughing. 'I thought they were coming for me again!', he said. It was a reference to his previous arrest in London during an immigration enforcement operation in Victoria Station. It was this arrest, for not having a valid UK visa, that set him on a course of a life in immigration removal centres, couch surfing, sleeping rough and living in the night shelters. It was a reminder that even in the relatively safe and otherwise welcoming space of the library, amid monotonous days book-ended by entering and leaving the shelters, there was a constant anxiety about the very real threat of border enforcement.

'It's the city's living room', one of Manchester Central Library's Customer Service Managers said to me during an interview in 2015.

We were sitting in the ground floor cafe of the newly refurbished and reopened Central Library and I had just asked her how she would define the library as a space. 'To be honest with you, I don't know who came up with that quote', she continued, 'but I quote it now because that's basically what it is – it's the city's living room. It's supposed to be an open and free space for people to come in and meet friends. If they want to join the library they're more than welcome to'. The Customer Service Manager could very well have been referring to the 2002 study on the Toronto Reference Library and Vancouver Public Library by Gloria Leckie and Jeffrey Hopkins. According to Leckie and Hopkins, for many users who visited on a daily or weekly basis, the libraries 'served as an extension of their living room' (Leckie and Hopkins, 2002: p. 353). Along with earlier studies Leckie and Hopkins have emphasised the public library's potential for becoming a multifaceted public space where people are free to come and go at their leisure, regardless of social status, and where knowledge is made accessible to 'all publics' (Lees, 1997: p. 344; Greenlagh and Worpole, 1995: p. 12; Leckie and Hopkins, 2002: p. 360). Each of these studies is tempered by the recognition that the increasing privatisation of public libraries can potentially lead to differential forms of paid access to services, and that libraries are necessarily surveilled spaces, where staff or private security guards may regulate behaviour that is deemed disruptive – as I discovered while sleeping at the table – or remove individuals from the space (Lees, 1997: pp. 336, 339, 344; Leckie and Hopkins, 2002: p. 360).

Earlier in this book, I introduced the notion of 'spaces of asylum' which I defined broadly as the spaces where the legal and social processes of asylum policy are played out and acted upon. This definition carried both affirmative 'political' meanings associated with refuge, sanctuary, agency, and individual and collective potential, as well as more negative meanings associated with constraint, indignity, and depreciating rights. Manchester Central Library can be considered as a more affirmative, and indeed political, space of asylum as individuals and groups living under the socio-legal conditions of being an asylum seeker, refused asylum seeker or refugee can spend their day in a safe, warm and non-judgemental environment, and can access library services without questions about their background or legal status. As the Customer Services Manager pointed out, an individual can sign up for a library card without being asked for a proof of address. During the interview the Customer Services Manager also pointed me to a statement released by the Society of Chief Librarians which affirmed that 'public libraries are safe, trusted spaces and are able to offer a range of vital services for new arrivals in local communities across the country' (Association of Senior Children's and Education Librarians, 2015). The statement was timed in response to the UK Government's announcement in 2015 that 20,000 Syrian refugees would be received by the UK over the next five years. While offering welcome, practical and free support to the 'new arrivals', the Society also took its statement further by declaring that 'this welcome is also extended to the existing 150,000 refugees, asylum seekers, and stateless people who are currently in the country'. It concluded by referencing occasions when public libraries had been used by refused asylum seekers to gather fresh material and information to support successful appeals against negative decisions by the UK Government. The statement aimed to break down forms of differential inclusion by reaffirming equality of access to library services, something which was played out during my time with Victor and others in Manchester Central Library. It was a direct challenge to the UK's hostile policy environment towards asylum seekers. The library was a 'space of asylum', in an open and welcoming sense, beyond the strict binaries of exclusion and inclusion. It was a space of overlapping meanings, uses and practices as people used the library as a space to spend time, study and learn, connect to the internet and stay safe and warm.

The definition of 'spaces of asylum' I am offering, however, is not reducible to specific sites or discrete spaces, but also includes anywhere the border was borne by the legal-social status of individuals. 'Spaces of asylum' include areas and places across the city that are inscribed and re-inscribed with meaning by those facing destitution and living under the label of asylum seeker, refused asylum seeker or refugee.[1] Chorlton Street Coach Station serves as an example. On that early morning in December, Hani, Naveed, Wasim, Yevgeny and I were not waiting for a bus or there to pick somebody up. Instead, we were simply using the space to see out the day in a warm and relatively safe environment. The waiting area of the intercity coach station had become a sort of 'living room' for us – in a similar manner to how the Customer Services

Manager had described the library. The station was busy with traffic and travellers and Wasim made a point of greeting the station employees who passed by our seats, whether security guards, coach drivers or cleaners. They were simple greetings – a mere 'hello' and a nod, a 'good morning', or 'having good day, mate?' – and served the strategic purpose of creating a rapport with those working in the station in order to make our presence more acceptable.

The five of us would spend the hours shifting between silence and conversation, talking about everything from religion and our families, to imagining our lives if we all moved to Dubai together. Wasim would also, occasionally, make his way out of the station and onto the street to ask people for cigarettes. These long hours of shooting the breeze, of talking and silence, and of sitting stationary in relatively comfortable spaces, were typical of many of the spaces in which we spent our time – whether the communal area of the Boaz Trust offices, the coach station, or the library.

Like others in the night shelters, Wasim, Hani and Naveed also passed their time in different bookmakers and casinos around the city centre. Casinos had become particularly important places for Wasim to see out his days while living in the shelters and, prior to that, living on the street. Using the right tactics, he would tell me, a person could spend a day in a casino without attracting attention or spending money. He would never spend consecutive days in the same casino and would slip into a toilet cubicle to sleep, out of sight from the CCTV cameras. He had shared this advice with Hani when he arrived in the night shelters and the two would move around the different casinos in Chinatown together.

In a recorded interview, Danny spoke about his time living in the Boaz Trust night shelters and how we would often spend his days sitting in a bookmakers. Danny was originally from Zimbabwe and had stayed in the Boaz Trust night shelters over the course of two winter seasons. He reflected on the night shelters and his time on the street over a cup of coffee at the Nexus Art Cafe, below the Methodist Central Hall in Manchester's Northern Quarter. Although Danny remained a refused asylum seeker nearly a decade after his asylum claim was first rejected, he had recently found stable accommodation through the network of supporters and contacts he had developed over the years. When I asked him where he usually spent his days while living in the shelters, Danny replied that he stayed in the bookies or in the library, emphasising that 'the bookies are the best place'. 'It was always warm in a bookies', he said adding, 'the football is on. You just sit there and relax, like you're watching football, and then you go to sleep'. Despite never placing a bet, Danny said he was never bothered by the staff while spending his hours in a bookmaker's shop. 'As long as you keep yourself clean and don't look bad, they just assume you're tired', he said. 'You're not drunk, you're not causing problems. Normally they'll just look at you and give you the benefit of the doubt'. Like the library and like the coach station, the bookmakers had become a 'living room' of sorts for Danny.

To be 'out of place' – to return to Talmadge Wright's phrase – can sometimes necessitate discrete practices of 'making place', however temporary, whether in the library or coach station or bookmakers. For the men in the night shelters, such practices are ways of passing time. Spaces of asylum hold tensions between movement and fixity, agency and restriction and however much new meanings are inscribed, and re-inscribed into these spaces, and however much the binary of inclusion and exclusion may momentarily melt away, there remains the underlying condition of doubled placelessness and the idleness, boredom and frustrations that accompany it.

Note

1 In their 2008 study of homelessness in Bristol, UK, Cloke, May, and Johnsen argue that notions of the homeless city cannot be reduced to binaries of inclusion and exclusion or determined by regulations and controls, but also involve the ways in which people experiencing homelessness themselves inscribe and re-inscribe meanings to the urban environment. This point was essential to my understanding of 'spaces of asylum' as also being areas where those living under the social-legal condition of 'refused asylum seeker' create and inscribe their own meanings to different spaces (Cloke, May and Johnsen, 2008).

2

Ethnography in a hostile environment

In search of respect

In his work *In Search of Respect*, Phillipe Bourgois introduces the reader to his research with young Puerto Rican crack dealers in 1990s' New York by retelling the moment he disrespected a crack-house owner by accidently exposing him as an illiterate in front of his crew. This *faux pas* not only threatened his continued research, but also his physical safety. It also reinforced the need to follow certain, unwritten codes of respect within his research (Bourgois, 2003: pp. 20–2). In this chapter I begin with my own *faux pas* – my own mistake.

It occurred while I was walking along Oxford Road with Wasim and Naveed in early December 2013 as we saw out the day waiting for the next shelter to open. We happened to see a sight-impaired man waiting at a crosswalk and Wasim walked over to offer a hand. It turned out the man, whose name was Henry, spoke fluent Arabic and as the four of us continued along the busy road Wasim and Henry struck up a long conversation. Henry then invited us to sit with him in a cafe outside Oxford Road Station as he waited for his train to Liverpool. At the cafe, Henry turned to me and asked who I was and where I was from. I said I was a researcher in London. During my time on the streets with the men staying in the shelters, I would often introduce myself to strangers in such vague terms and leave it at that. But Henry took an immediate interest in the fact that I was a researcher and with Wasim and Naveed on either side of me, began to earnestly question me: 'What are you researching?', 'What theories are you using?', 'What examples are you using?'. I was caught off guard by his persistence and said I was staying in the night shelters with Wasim and Naveed. It was only later that I realised what I had done.

As we saw Henry off on his train and left the station, Wasim roughly barged into me with his shoulder, knocking me momentarily off balance. 'You didn't need to tell him that I'm in the shelters. You brought shame on me, Mark. That's why I left the cafe'. Wasim hadn't gone out for a cigarette earlier as I had thought, but instead had left out of embarrassment at my disclosure. I apologised to Wasim there and then. And did so later that evening. He told me not to worry: 'Henry is a good man and he wouldn't care'. The implication was that others would care. And Wasim certainly did care. And for reasons entirely different to Wasim, I felt shame at my own carelessness.

Shame is a complex emotion. It cannot be pinned down as being exclusively negative or positive, damaging or constructive. According to Jean-Paul Sartre, shame reveals the fundamental ontological structure of the human being which is an inescapable relation to others. Through his dictum 'I am ashamed *of* myself *before* the Other', Sartre argues that shame is the recognition that I am always already caught up in the other's gaze (Sartre, 2003: pp. 246, 296). Drawing on Sartre, the philosopher Lisa Guenther writes that shame is a notoriously ambivalent notion (2011: p. 22). It is, she argues, indispensable to ethical life – our life together – as it constitutes a person's openness and vulnerability to others. Shame can be ethically provocative as it can shake us out of our complacency regarding another's social situation, yet it can also be used to exert control, to normalise exclusion and reinforce patterns of silencing. The moment on Oxford Road exemplified this ambivalence. Wasim was shamed by my thoughtless disclosure of his legal status and destitution while I was shamed into recognising that even the most prosaic response to a stranger's questions could be deeply disrespectful and unethical in such a context.

Awkward and uneasy situations are an almost unavoidable part of ethnographic practice. Such moments, like the one I have described on Oxford Road, can lead to heightened feelings of guilt and failure on the part of the researcher. Yet at the same time they can also illuminate the bumpy social textures of research practice and the political and cultural landscape in which it takes place. These moments can be both troubling and revelatory. The anthropologists Lynne

Hume and Jane Mulcock argue that participant observation – a central practice of ethnographic research – is fraught with inconsistency and ambiguity (2004: p. xii). The researcher must simultaneously position themselves as intellectually and analytically distant from the social situations and actions they are documenting as well as being deeply embedded in them. This requires a delicate balance between separation and belonging. Hume and Mulcock call this the 'insider-outsider' dilemma (2004: p. xix). It is an emotionally charged position as a range of feelings emerge and submerge over the course of any ethnographic research project.

In this respect, rather than being mere psychological states or something that individual researchers, participants and informants possess, emotions are both embodied and social, as Sara Ahmed writes (2004). They accrue meaning and value through their circulation in and across media, social relations, policy and research. Loosened from atomistic understandings, this 'sociality of emotions' (p. 8) is multi-layered as emotions flow between and through the micro and macro. The moment on Oxford Road not only speaks to the relationship between Wasim and I, but also a research context which is shaped by wider feelings of hostility and suspicion directed at racialised migrants and people experiencing homelessness. Such feelings are formed and enacted through policy and practice to the extent that they can be declared in official agendas such as the 'hostile environment'.

Emotions are complicated, messy, politicised and ambivalent. They can be intense and in their circulation they can take on different meanings for different people, depending on who you are and your social and legal status. For this reason, attention to the emotional landscape of ethnography is important as it raises a number of methodological concerns. Emotions cut right through the formal boundaries of ethnographic research: the boundaries between the field and everyday life, between researcher and informant, between the personal and the political, between data gathering and analysis and between immediate experience and the more reflective work of writing. A multitude of emotions and feelings run through this ethnography alongside refused, destitute asylum seekers: hope and despair, respect and shame, dignity and indignity, love and anger, joy and sorrow, hostility and care. They do so at different scales, from the organisational to the individual and from state policy formation through to grassroots actions.

Emotions can also have a transformative role in research. They can be both disturbing and productive, not only providing insight into the political and cultural terrain of ethnographic work within the Boaz Trust night shelters and on the streets of Manchester, but also my own position within this research. This chapter weaves together policy, methodology and personal reflection on faith and practice. Underlying these reflections is the realisation that restless justice is necessarily an emotional task as it involves partisan engagement with unjust systems while striving to articulate a different order of things whether through the mobile solidarities of the night shelters or the act of writing itself.

Control

The research informing this book was carried out during a period of toxic ideological struggle within the UK. On 23 June 2016, the UK voted via a national referendum to leave the European Union, a departure that was formalised nearly four years later on 31 January 2020. The UK's exit from the EU and the passionate and ongoing debate surrounding it exposed deep political and social fractures within the nation. It exposed generational divides and fissures between major metropolitan centres and peripheral towns and the countryside. It also exposed regional differences and entrenched divisions between internal nationalisms within the UK as Scotland and Northern Ireland voted overwhelmingly to remain in the EU while England and Wales voted to leave. These divisions often overlapped with each other and although they existed before Brexit, they were also exacerbated by it.

A key issue informing the decision to leave the EU was that of immigration. It dominated political discourse and public life leading up to the referendum, in sometimes violent ways. On the same day that Nigel Farage, then leader of the anti-EU UK Independence Party, unveiled a campaign poster depicting a long queue of Syrian refugees crossing the Slovenian border under the caption 'Breaking Point', a neo-Nazi assassinated the pro-refugee Labour Member of Parliament, Jo Cox, on a street in the Yorkshire town of Batley after reportedly shouting the fascist slogan 'Britain First!'. On that same day, 16 June 2016, footage also emerged of England football supporters openly mocking refugee children in the streets of Lille, France, during the 2016 European Football Championship.

These incidents were all separate, but at the same time they were also all connected. They were all, in part, the product of years of anti-immigrant rhetoric circulating within the UK and years of restrictive immigration policies and practices taken up by successive UK governments, both Labour and Conservative. Vote Leave was the official campaign behind the drive to leave the EU in the lead up to the referendum. Their slogan was 'Take Control' which was then applied to a range of issues including the UK border, under the assumption that the UK had somehow lost control of its borders (Vote Leave, 2016).

Yet, the idea of taking back control of the border was a prominent theme in UK political discourse long before this and has continued to this day. The *Fairer, Faster, Firmer* white paper released by the government under Prime Minister Tony Blair in 1998 focused on 'immigration controls' and made continual reference to 'genuine asylum seekers' and 'abusive claimants', asserting a moral distinction between the good migrant and the bad migrant, casting lives as wanted and unwanted, deserving and undeserving (Home Office, 1998). The document laid the foundations for a complete reorganisation of the UK asylum system through the 1999 Immigration and Asylum Act at the opening of the twenty-first century, establishing dispersal, weaponised time, enforced destitution and denial as key pillars of deterrence and control within the UK asylum regime that have remained in place over the quarter of a century since.

Dispersal and weaponised time

Returning to the stories of the men staying in the night shelters can serve to articulate these four pillars of dispersal, weaponised time, destitution and denial. As described in the Chapter 1, Salah had claimed asylum while studying at a university in London. He was moved into National Asylum Support Service (NASS) accommodation in Manchester while his claim was processed and eventually rejected. Like many others seeking protection in the UK, Salah had been relocated to a different area of the UK on a no-choice basis. Under the 1999 Immigration and Asylum Act, people claiming asylum became subject to compulsory dispersal to towns and cities across the country. Denied the right to work, asylum seekers also receive a cash allowance (via a government issued card) of £49.18 a week while their claims are assessed, which is well below the standard £92.05 a week available through Job Seeker's Allowance (HM Government, 2025).[1]

NASS was effectively set up at the opening of the twenty-first century to remove asylum seekers from mainstream welfare support through an alternative, but degraded system. While the stated rationale behind dispersal was to ease the supposed strain that people seeking asylum placed on housing and services in London and the South East of England as well as discourage the long-term settlement of refugees in these areas, the policy was also shaped by economic opportunism and the availability of cheap and vacant housing in areas across Scotland, Wales, the Midlands and North of England, including Greater Manchester. Dispersal therefore typically involves relocating vulnerable populations to towns and cities with existing social deprivation and poverty (Bloch and Schuster, 2005; Zetter, Griffiths and Sigona, 2005: p. 171; Schuster, 2005: p. 617; Phillimore and Goodson, 2006: pp. 1715–7; Phillips, 2006: p. 542; Gill, 2009: p. 187; Rainey, 2019a; Rainey, 2019b). The policy not only assumes that people seeking asylum are a burden on public services and consequently should be managed through compulsory relocation, but also constructs asylum seekers as transient and placeless figures, always on the move and disconnected from the communities in which they reside (Schuster, 2005: p. 608; Zetter, Griffiths and Sigona, 2005: p. 176; Gill, 2009: p. 187; Hynes, 2011; Squire, 2009: pp. 116–41; Darling, 2017: pp. 182–3; Rainey, 2019a; Rainey, 2019b; Darling, 2023).

Following the rejection of his asylum claim, Salah had twenty-one days to vacate his NASS accommodation and was expected to leave the country. Fearing for his safety upon returning to Egypt and facing the prospect of street homelessness in the UK, Salah presented himself to the offices of Refugee Action in Manchester who then referred him on to the Boaz Trust who offered him a place in the night shelters. He would spend the next five months living in the network, sleeping on a different church floor each night of the week. As the night shelters closed for the winter, Salah would be moved into hosted accommodation arranged by the Boaz Trust where he lived with a local family in south Manchester and later into Boaz Trust housing where he lived with other men whose claims for asylum had also been refused. It was during this time Salah worked on a judicial review of his asylum claim. Over the following months and years Salah would move between different housing in Manchester, his situation unresolved.

The story of Victor was also introduced in Chapter 1. He had arrived in the Boaz Trust night shelters after sleeping rough in central Manchester following three weeks couch-surfing at a friend's place after being released from Harmondsworth Immigration Removal Centre. He claimed asylum after being arrested during an immigration enforcement operation in Victoria Station London after his Visitor's Visa had expired. His claim for asylum was 'fast-tracked' while in detention. This was 'quite frustrating', he would tell me, as he did not have the means or time to gather evidence that would support his claim. As Saulo Cwerner writes, the fast-tracking of asylum claims effectively silences and obliterates the temporal complexities of the refugee experience (2004: p. 73). Alongside restricted access to outside information while incarcerated, Victor was given little opportunity to discuss his case with the legal representation provided to him. Sometimes he would meet with his designated lawyer only fifteen minutes prior to an interview with immigration officials while other times they would not be available at all. Both Victor's asylum application and appeal were rejected while in detention. After five months Victor was released without explanation and returned to Manchester where he had previously been staying, only to find that a 'friend' had sold all his possessions. Destitute, Victor presented himself to a refugee support charity in the city who referred him on to the Boaz Trust. He spent the next six months living in the shelter network before moving into shared housing provided by the Boaz Trust while he put together a fresh asylum claim. Over the coming years Victor would move between different accommodation around the city with the support of friends and refugee activists, until his eventual arrest, detention and deportation from the UK.

Temir arrived in the night shelters in early 2013, around the same time as Salah. Originally from Iraq, Temir had lived and worked in the UK as an irregular migrant before claiming asylum. He was placed in NASS accommodation in Manchester while his claim was assessed and rejected. Like Salah and Victor, Temir ended up staying in the Boaz Trust night shelters and over the next four months moved between churches and slept on a different floor each night. As the night shelters were closing after the 2013 winter season, Temir faced the prospect of street homelessness as there were no spaces available in the Boaz Trust's housing or hosted accommodation. Temir applied for temporary state support under section 4 of the 1999 Immigration and Asylum Act and was later relocated to NASS accommodation in Northampton.

Section 4 support is a 'last resort' for many refused asylum seekers (Independent Asylum Commission, 2008: p. 2; Lewis, 2009: § 2.3.2; British Red Cross and Boaz Trust, 2013: p. 5; Rowlands, 2019: pp. 24 and 48–9; Rainey, 2019a). It offers no-choice accommodation and voucher payments of £49.81 a week to those who 'appear to be destitute' and are 'taking all reasonable steps to leave the UK' but are unable to do so whether for medical reasons or because there is no lawful or viable route of return (Home Office, 2022). Due to the eligibility requirements, claims for this support necessarily take place from a position of homelessness and claimants must agree to return to their countries of origin when it is safe and legal to do so. As the experience of Temir indicates, accessing section 4 support also often requires further compulsory relocation. In this respect, it keeps people in a condition of prolonged temporariness, without formal recognition as a refugee, unable to work and always expected to leave the country.

The three men, like many others who would stay in the Boaz Trust night shelters, were subject to what Jonathan Darling refers to as the 'slow violence' of the asylum system (2023). This is a distributed violence that is social, spatial and temporal. It involves being caught up in hostile bureaucratic processes that both speed up and slow down as well as enforced movement through the vagaries of the dispersal system and the accompanying isolation and marginalisation faced by asylum seekers as they are cast as burdens on society and the communities in which they are placed. It is a system that utilises time as a weapon to exhaust applicants and make their lives miserable while still meeting the UK's basic commitments under international law and the 1951 Refugee Convention. For Victor, Temir, Salah and many others, prolonged periods of waiting are punctuated by forced and sudden change. For some there is still hope of obtaining refugee status, while for others this hope fades further and further from view or is completely foreclosed.

Over their time in the UK each had undergone significant shifts in status – whether from undocumented migrant, international student or visitor to asylum seeker and refused asylum seeker – with the differing rights, restrictions and exposure to border enforcement that each entailed. People seeking asylum in the UK often find themselves subject to a seemingly endless state of waiting and anxious expectation and an important assertion here is that the UK asylum system, glimpsed in the stories and experiences of the men living in the night shelters, utilises what I have termed the 'weaponisation of time' (Rainey, 2019a). This describes the ways in which the Home Office seeks to control the temporal experiences of asylum seekers in an attempt to demean, frustrate, exhaust and punish individuals. The term was first used by Nina Power in her reflections on the UK's criminal justice system as the slowness of bringing someone to trial and the trial process itself stretches time out in a manner that punishes people even before it penalises them (2014). Developed further here in the context of the UK asylum system, the weaponisation of time is not only the extension of time but its curtailment – from protracted periods of stasis to a sudden change in legal status or compelled relocation and even arrest and incarceration. This weaponisation of time is the temporal dimension of the slow violence of the asylum system. It carries an elasticity that stretches out, but also snaps back like a rubber band. It is activated through policy and practice and sits alongside other institutionally embedded deterrents such as dispersal, detention and the threat of deportation which are ostensibly used to discourage people from making claims for protection in the UK and encourage people to return to their country of origin. This weaponised time has been built into the asylum system over decades. Yet, as the resilience of the men staying in the shelters indicates, these mechanisms often fail in their official purpose and more accurately function as forms of retaliation for the very act of claiming asylum in the UK.

Destitution and denial

With the introduction of compulsory dispersal and the establishment of NASS, the 1999 Immigration and Asylum Act fundamentally changed how the UK engaged with people seeking asylum. As the stories of Temir, Salah and Victor indicate, both dispersal and the broader support system are structured in such a way that many asylum seekers are pushed into destitution and unable to meet their most basic needs including food, shelter and safety. Although destitution may be experienced throughout the asylum claims process, particularly if NASS support is withdrawn or delayed, most reported destitution occurs once an initial decision has been made (Lewis, 2009: § 2; British Red Cross and Boaz Trust, 2013: p. 5; Crawley, Hemmings and Price, 2011: p. 16; Rainey, 2019a; Rainey, 2019b, Wheeler, 2024). Those who are granted refugee status or other forms of protection must vacate their accommodation within 28 days and are expected to find employment and housing or access mainstream welfare support through the local authority where they reside. Many find it difficult to do so within such a short period of time and experience temporary homelessness as a result. Some of the men using the shelters have moved from other towns and cities to Manchester to find work, housing and community and rely on the spaces as temporary accommodation while they restart their lives (Stewart and Shaffer, 2015: p. 35). Those who have had their claims refused must leave their accommodation within 21 days and are expected to leave the country. Many are unable and/or unwilling to do so and become reliant on others for support. The Independent Asylum Commission has termed this embedded threat of homelessness as an 'enforced destitution' (2008: p. 2).

Alongside dispersal, weaponised time and destitution is a long-standing culture of denial within the asylum system (Refugee Action, 2006: p. 58; Joseph Rowntree Charitable Trust, 2007: p. 7; Independent Asylum Commission, 2008: p. 2; Rowlands, 2019: p. 13; Rainey, 2019b). Prior to the global COVID-19 pandemic, including the years in which this research was undertaken, the majority of asylum claims were rejected in the first instance.[2] For example, in 2018, 67 per cent of the 21,119 initial decisions were refusals. This was a similar percentage to the years 2016 and 2017 and part of a much wider trend dating back almost three decades (Refugee Council, 2019). Behind this culture of denial is the abiding belief that the majority of people claiming asylum are not genuine. As Bohmer and Shuman write, 'the fear of the bogus asylum seeker permeates the system to the detriment of genuine asylum seekers. Asylum seekers are guilty until proven innocent' (Bohmer and Shuman, 2008: p. 11). Although people who have had their applications refused are able to appeal the decision, this process continues an often, already prolonged engagement with the asylum system and the social and legal uncertainty this entails – another feature of its slow violence.

There are no official records on the number of refused and destitute asylum seekers living in the UK and estimates vary widely. However, the British Red Cross and Boaz Trust suggested in 2013 that there may be more than 2,000 refused asylum seekers living in Greater Manchester with 300–400 people accessing refugee and asylum seeker support services across the city each week (2013: pp. 7, 11). In its 2006 report, written seven years after the 1999 Immigration and Asylum Act gave shape to the contemporary asylum regime, Refugee Action remarked that,

> [...] there exists in Britain a new and growing excluded class of people whose asylum applications have been refused, who are afraid or unable to return to their countries of origin, who have no contact with authorities, no access to work or mainstream support services, and little prosect of their situation being resolved (Refugee Action, 2006: p. 2)

Nearly two decades on, individuals continue to face destitution and prolonged legal and social uncertainty on account of their immigration status. Yet, rather than seeing in official measures that would alleviate this crisis, we are witnessing the ratcheting up of hostility towards this excluded class of people in political discourse and policy.

Hostility

Over the past forty years, UK asylum policy has followed a trajectory of increased restrictions, depreciating rights and securitisation (Philo, Briant and Donald, 2013: pp. 19–28; Darling, 2011: p. 264; Squire, 2009: p. 116; Rainey, 2019a). Alongside the creation of NASS with its programme of compulsory dispersal and the removal of the right to work for asylum claimants in 2002, the UK also introduced indefinite detention for those found in breach of immigration rules. This increasingly restrictive policy landscape has been coupled with anti-immigrant discourse in the media and across the political spectrum, from politicians such as former Prime Minister David Cameron referring to irregular migrants arriving from Calais, France as a 'swarm' invading the country (Elgot and Taylor, 2015) through to the infamous coffee mugs issued by the Labour Party during the 2015 general election that promised 'controls on immigration' (Perraudin, 2015). Former Prime Minister Boris Johnson erroneously warned that the Roman Empire fell because of 'uncontrolled immigration' as it could 'no longer control its borders' (Walker, 2021; Fafinski, 2021) while current Prime Minister Sir Keir Starmer stated that without reductions to immigration Britain would become an 'island of strangers', echoing the words of the anti-immigrant politician Enoch Powell and his 1968 'Rivers of Blood' speech (Walker, 2025). While these examples only sketch the rhetoric appearing within mainstream political discourse, such comments are indicative of how anti-immigrant and anti-asylum discourse is embedded within contemporary UK politics.

When then Home Secretary and future Prime Minister Theresa May publicly announced her intention to create a 'really hostile environment' for so-called 'illegal immigrants' in 2012 she was essentially giving name to an abiding atmosphere within mainstream politics and a long-standing set of policies and practices within the UK asylum and immigration system (Kirkup and Winnet, 2012; Goodfellow, 2019; Rainey, 2019a). Her explicit use of the term 'illegal immigrant' amounted to the raising of a contemporary 'folk-devil' (Cohen, 2011) which was then accompanied by a combined media and legislative agenda. The accompanying 2014 and 2016 Immigration Acts included measures to isolate irregular migrants by restricting access to housing, healthcare and bank accounts as well as extending the financial and custodial penalties for working without proper documentation or employing someone who does not have the right to work in the UK, effectively placing members of the public on the frontline of immigration enforcement (Rowlands, 2019: pp. 45–50; Jones *et al.*, 2017: p. 6; Bowling and Westenra, 2018; Rainey, 2019b). Yuval-Davis, Wemyss and Cassidy refer to this as 'everyday bordering' and it has not only become a mainstay of law and policy but an increasingly normal and accepted part of social life (2018).

In the year leading up to the legislation, Home Office adverts appeared in primarily Black, Asian and minority ethnic newspapers warning those without leave to remain in the UK to return home or face arrest. Immigration raids by the Home Office were posted on social media and two vans were driven around six of the most ethnically diverse areas of London carrying billboards that read, 'In the UK illegally? GO HOME OR FACE ARREST'. As Jones *et al.* write, the vans seemed to mark a turning point in the climate of immigration debate within the UK as government-sponsored advertisements had adopted the abusive language of far-right racists (2017: p. 3).

Although the 'hostile environment' came under sustained criticism following the Windrush scandal in which British subjects of Caribbean origin were wrongfully denied housing and healthcare and subject to detention and deportation (House of Lords, 2018; Bowling and Westenra, 2018; Rainey, 2019a) and the phrase was dropped from official use, immigration and asylum policy has continued on a trajectory of outright hostility to irregular migrants.

Indeed, in his foreword to the 2025 *Restoring Control of the Immigration System* white paper, Keir Starmer makes the exaggerated claim that the UK has become a 'one-nation experiment in open borders' which has done 'incalculable' damage to the country (Home Office, 2025b: p. 3). The proposed corresponding legislation under the Border Security, Asylum and Immigration Bill frames irregular migration as a national security issue. While it repeals the previous government's Safety of Rwanda (Immigration and Asylum) Act 2024 and aspects of the Illegal Migration Act 2023 which effectively barred people arriving in the UK via irregular means from claiming protection and mandated their detention and eventual deportation to third countries such as Rwanda, it continues to emphasise notions of 'control' by creating new criminal offences for supplying articles and information used for 'illegal entry' and 'unlawful immigration' to the UK. Importantly, the repeal of the Safety of Rwanda (Immigration and Asylum) Act 2024 was on the grounds of cost and unworkability rather than humanitarian concern and the UK Government continues to seek out third countries to act as 'return hubs' for those who have had their claims for asylum refused in the UK (Courea, 2024; Adu, Syal and Walker, 2025).

Faith and the field

In the autumn of 2009 my grandfather visited Manchester from Western Canada. It was a journey he had made many times over the decades to visit family who had immigrated to the UK. He was 90 years-old at the time and said this visit would be his last. One afternoon my grandfather, Mum and I made a trip to Quarry Bank Mill near Styal, Cheshire. It's a National Trust site just outside the city. We spent the afternoon at the historic cotton mill before driving back to Manchester. On the way home my mum made an unannounced detour and pulled up at the gates of Styal Women's Prison. As we sat in the car, she began talking to us about a young mother who was locked up inside.

The woman was a member of the Longsight Community Church (LCC) that my mother and other members of our immediate and extended family attended. She was originally from central Africa and had been living and working in the UK for a number of years and was involved in the church community. She also had a three-year-old daughter. The young mother had been arrested for overstaying her visa and working without permission. She was now incarcerated inside and separated from her child. In a show of solidarity and support other women in the church began to schedule visits to the prison each week, spending time with their friend inside. The full force of the UK border regime had been deployed against a member of the community and the situation had a deep impact on people like my mother. It would not be the last time a member of the church would be arrested and detained by immigration authorities.

It was not long after this that my mum suggested I volunteer in the Friday night shelter for refused and destitute asylum seekers at the LCC. A year earlier the Boaz Trust had established the shelter network in seven churches across the city and the LCC was among the first to join. The LCC belongs to the Church of the Nazarene, an international evangelical denomination in the Methodist tradition. Although the LCC traces its roots back to Victorian-era industrial Manchester, its current building and location date to 1985. The church is located in Longsight, an ethnically diverse, working-class area of inner-city Manchester that has served, along with the surrounding areas of Rusholme and Levenshulme, as an entry point for migrants from around the world over the past two centuries.

Much of the participant observation informing this book took place in the Friday night shelter and among the volunteers and church community at the LCC. It is an 'outward-looking' church listing 'justice', 'inclusion' and 'compassion' among its core passions which informed not only the night shelter but other community engagement activities such as the Longsight and Ardwick Food Bank, hosting a community cafe and allotment (Longsight Community Church of the Nazarene, 2025). I have long-standing connections to the church and the wider denomination it belongs to. My immediate and extended family regularly attend the LCC and have held both voluntary and paid leadership roles. Indeed, many of my immediate and extended family – both women and men in Canada and the UK – are ordained ministers, theologians, educators and lay leaders within the Church of the Nazarene.

All of this is to say that I was raised in the Church of the Nazarene, although I no longer attend an evangelical church. My relationship with this branch of Christianity can be described as ambiguous at best, balancing an ongoing connection rooted in family history and community practice alongside a deep-seated revulsion at the broader social and political conservatism and bigotry that often dominates evangelicalism, although not the LCC in particular. I tend to keep a healthy distance from it all. Yet, over the course of my years volunteering in the LCC, I also became attracted to the faith-based social and ethical commitments of the church and the Boaz Trust more widely. Conducting research in the night shelters, alongside a diverse group of volunteers, was an encounter with the 'theo-ethical' and a prophetic radicalism that sought to enact transformative change in the community and city whether through the weekly night shelter or activating networks of solidarity for those under threat from the border regime. The work done in the night shelters eschewed traditional approaches to Christian charity that placed emphasis on conversion and proselytising, in favour of a theo-ethical engagement with the community, creating 'mobile solidarities' in which cultural categories and legal distinctions disappear or are rendered unimportant. As I witnessed a modelling of a version of the Kingdom of God in the here and now, my research drew me closer to the faith in which I was raised, but this time through re-politicised Christian notions of love and justice. Volunteering in the shelters over the years coincided with a deeper participation in the LCC overall, regularly attending its worship services.

The writer Jennifer C. Martin introduced the term 'Dirtbag Christian' to describe her journey away from evangelical Christianity while maintaining her faith (2020) and perhaps this is a useful descriptor of my own transformed position. The notion regards essential Christian practice as the desire for the overthrow of empires and the pushing forth of the marginalised and abandoned. It is a faith motivated by the radical figure of Christ and a vision of the Kingdom of God in which the 'last will be first, and the first will be last' (Matthew 20:16). It is faith expressed as a theo-ethical practice. It is being situated within present conditions while drawing on notions of Christian love and justice to actively challenge them. It is a 'restless justice' on personal and social level, with all the perplexities, emotional challenges and ambiguities, weaknesses, mistakes, joys and sorrows that this entails.

My personal and family connections with the Church of the Nazarene and LCC coupled with my re-engagement with Christianity along more politicised – or dirtbag – lines meant that using the night shelters as a site of research was an anxious and ambiguous mix of ease and unease. Unease because the formal boundaries between the so-called 'field' and my personal life were constantly blurred as I was volunteering and conducting research alongside friends, acquaintances and family. In the night shelters and other spaces, the distinction between research and social life fell apart. And more than this, the shelters became spaces of a continual reconfiguring of my own understanding of Christian faith. There was also a certain sense of ease because I was familiar with the faith-based idiom often used by Boaz Trust employees and shelter volunteers, whether in their references to Christian love and justice or to particular stories and passages from the Bible when talking about their motivations for working in the shelters. Participating in these discourses was not merely a means to advance discussion during interviews and conversations but would also – and much more importantly – inform my emerging theo-ethical understanding of the practices that were taking place in the shelters. In the shelters, faith-talk was accompanied by community action.

That said, people of no faith and different faiths were also involved in the night shelters. As focal points of service provision on the frontline of a crisis facing people seeking asylum in Manchester, those wanting to address community issues and work in support of asylum seekers were drawn to the shelters. Many of the volunteers working at the LCC over the years were students and international students studying at the city's universities. As one international student from Spain explained to me one evening as we volunteered together in the night shelter, he wanted to 'give something back' to the city before returning home after his studies. Other volunteers were colleagues or friends of LCC members or friends of friends. Others were local residents who recognised the church's activities as a way of supporting their community. The LCC drew in a wide network of people of different ages and backgrounds who not only kept the shelter running, but also gained a sense of personal development in return.

Extended place method

Carlos was the night shelter coordinator at the LCC during the early years of my research. Like myself, he was a migrant to the UK and I had known him for some time through our shared social circles. Originally from Colombia, he had lived in Spain before settling in Manchester where he became an ordained minister in the Church of the Nazarene and took up a leadership position at the LCC. His responsibilities as the shelter coordinator included recruiting and organising volunteers, organising shelter supplies and organising transport to and from Manchester city centre every Friday night. He was also a liaison between the Boaz Trust and LCC.

Carlos was keen to support my research and began to schedule me as a regular night shelter volunteer. Although I was living in London between 2011 and 2015, I would take the train to Manchester fortnightly during the winter or stay in the city for extended periods of time. Alongside my work in the shelters prior to beginning any formal research, this regular scheduling meant I was given more responsibility. On the Fridays I was volunteering I would be given keys to the church and most often be the first to arrive at the shelter and last to leave on Saturday morning. I often introduced new volunteers and new arrivals to the shelter and its routines and facilities. Although the role was very informal, acting as a sort of shelter manager meant I also took the lead in answering queries or concerns from volunteers or those staying in the shelters. I was also in direct contact with the Boaz Trust on Saturday mornings and would provide a list of names of the men who would need a place in the shelter that evening, as well as passing on any other important information. Carlos stepped down as the shelter coordinator in late 2016 and Zack, an American migrant to the UK who joined the leadership team of the LCC, took up the responsibility.

It was after discussions with Carlos and other leaders in the LCC in late 2011 that my research began to expand beyond the church. I met with the Projects Manager at the Boaz Trust to discuss the wider possibilities of this research project into the night shelters. What emerged was a programme of volunteering over multiple winter seasons, semi-structured interviews with volunteers, Boaz Trust employees and men staying in the shelters as well as three weeks spent living in the shelters, moving from venue to venue, alongside the men. This took my research across different venues in Greater Manchester: Emmanuel Church of the England in Didsbury on Monday nights, Heaton Park Methodist Church in Prestwich on Tuesday nights, St. Clements Church of England in Openshaw on Wednesday nights, Mount Chapel in Broughton, Salford on Thursday nights, the LCC on Friday nights, the South Manchester Family Church in Burnage on Saturday nights and the Ashton Church of the Nazarene in Ashton-Under-Lyne on Sunday nights. My involvement as an ethnographer was concentrated between 2011 and 2015 which were the formal years of my research project, but would also continue long after with my last work as a volunteer taking place in 2018.

Although the LCC and shelter network were the primary locations of this research, the ethnographic work extended beyond the shelters themselves and involved time on the streets as well as public and private spaces around the city such as Manchester Aquatics Centre, Manchester Central Library, casinos, transport stations, the Arndale Shopping Centre and refugee and homeless support services and drop-in spaces around the city. Mitch Duneier terms moving the fieldwork 'out' and across spaces in this way as an 'extended place method' (1999: p. 344). Time in the shelters became time on the streets and interviews with volunteers, support service employees, librarians and the men using the shelters took place in cafes, offices, homes, pubs, food banks and refugee and homeless support agencies in the city. Duneier links his 'extended place method' to the wider notion of 'multi-sited ethnography' (Marcus, 1995) which follows a research topic across multiple spaces, bringing together a variety of perspectives to understand a process, topic, or idea. It allows for an understanding of how institutions organise power and affect the various micro-settings that are studied. In this respect, departing from the micro-setting of the LCC to the macro-setting of the city offered an opportunity to gain a 'more rounded picture' (Duneier, 1999: p. 345) of the experience of those getting by on the streets and in the shelters and to critique the everyday effects of the social-legal category of 'refused asylum seeker', itself a product of the UK asylum system and wider processes of bordering.

The immigration line

In this book, I have suggested that the night shelters are 'spaces of asylum' or sites that are shaped by asylum policy and practice. Just as border processes are an intractable part of the night shelters, they are also an intractable part of the research process itself. The uniquity of borders not only exists in relation to the primacy spaces of this research – the shelters and the streets – but also in relation to research practice itself, to the very production of knowledge and the insider-outsider dilemma of ethnographic work highlighted by Hume and Mulcock. Categories such as 'researcher' and 'field' are neither neutral nor fixed. Drawing on WEB Du Bois' comment that the 'the problem of the twentieth century is the problem of the color-line' (Du Bois, 1989: p. 2), the sociologist Les Back suggests that the problem of the twenty-first century is the 'problem of the immigration line' (Back, 2007: pp. 11 and 31–2; see also Rainey, 2019a; Rainey, 2019b). Deeply implicated in racism's past and present, this problem names the ways in which thick social, legal and political lines are drawn through and across peoples of the world, designating those who can move freely across the globe and those who cannot and those who are endowed with the gift of citizenship and those whose lives are put on hold or cut short with impunity. The problem of the immigration line is the problem of differential inclusion as different people have varying experiences of, and exposure to, border regimes.

My position as a researcher is bound up with my own experiences as a transnational migrant. At the age of sixteen I moved with my family from rural, Western Canada to Manchester, UK. My teenage years were unsettled, moving between cultures and education systems, between the open landscape of the Canadian Prairie and the post-industrial English North and between the more globally accessible patterns of North American English to the broad and proud redoubt of the Manc accent and dialect. As an adult I chose to remain in the city. It had become my home. I studied European philosophy at Manchester Metropolitan University and worked for a number of years in the arts and cultural sector. In 2006 I became a British citizen, the only person in my immediate family to do so. I currently live between the west of Ireland and, for family reasons, Japan. As a white, English-speaking male, with dual citizenship between Canada and the UK, access to residency and employment rights across multiple countries in the 'global north' and passports and residency cards that allow relatively easy movement across multiple state borders, I am situated at the opposite end of the 'immigration line' to the men that lived day-to-day in the Boaz Trust night shelters.

The category of 'migrant' is wide. It covers the full spectrum of the 'immigration line' and is filled with individual histories and experiences. During my stays in the night shelter network, we were provided with transport from Manchester city centre to the next shelter every night of the week, usually around 9.00 pm. Often the transportation was a minibus operated by one of the churches, although sometimes it was a fleet of cars driven by volunteers. One evening as we were driven to the shelters, Victor and I sat together and, as we often did, got into a deep conversation. We spoke about my research and our own experiences as migrants to the UK and we talked about the privileges afforded to white Westerners arriving to the UK. Victor suggested that as a White Canadian I would always be welcome in the UK and had indeed been taken in as one of 'their own', while as a Black African, with a heavy accent, he could never expect to be fully accepted. There's a risk of overdetermining a single conversation in the back of a minibus, but these different experiences of inclusion and acceptance were made objective by the fundamental differences in our legal status. I was a migrant-become-citizen and Victor had recently had his asylum claim rejected. The path of inclusion open to me had eventually allowed me to take up funded research in a British university. While many of my rights to movement, employment and residency had extended over the years; those staying in the shelters had experienced a reduction in these same rights. I had opportunities to flourish in the UK while Victor's future in the country was brutally closed. The 'immigration line' and its historic and contemporary articulations through notions of race and nationality unavoidably cut through my research and my ability to move between spaces.

It is therefore important to recognise that the immigration line, as Les Back conceives it, is much more than a theoretical cipher to understand different phenomena within border and migration studies. It cuts through to the very heart of research practice and knowledge production. For Nicholas De Genova, a problem of ethnographic research is that it is often only made possible by social and institutional inequalities, particularly when it is framed along an inside-outside axis in which the researcher, from an imagined outside, discovers supposedly hidden truths of an exotic other (De Genova, 2007: pp. 21–2; Rainey, 2019a). Constituting irregular migrants as an object of study can easily result in researchers becoming agents in the production of a migrant's uneven social and legal status and become, in effect, 'accomplices to the discursive power of immigration law' (De Genova, 2002: pp. 422–3). It is necessary to recognise our own situatedness within institutional and social forms, so as to challenge, work through or dismantle them. This is the call of restless justice. It is also necessary to delineate the formation of contemporary immigration policy, including its emotional and political background. Terms such as asylum seeker, refused asylum seeker and refugee are buffeted and shaped by policy and practice. In other words, they need to be understood as active and contingent, rather than fixed labels to be taken at face value. It is only then that ethnographic work can critique these conditions so as to identify and transform them.

On the edge of the community of value

On a Saturday evening in late November 2013, we gathered around a table in a side room of the Kingsburn Hall night shelter in Burnage, south Manchester. Volunteers brought in plates of rice and curry that had been prepared in the building's kitchen, and the other men spending the night in the shelter and I began to eat our evening meal. As usual, conversations picked up around the table, often in multiple languages. Victor and I were sitting together and began talking. The topic eventually came around to my research and Victor asked me a provocative, personal question: 'Mark, what would you do if you worked in the Home Office?'. The question was informed by Victor's many personal encounters with border officials, whether in the police station, the detention centre, or the bus station in London where he was first arrested and it pressed home the issue of personal ethics in relation to employment in border enforcement and whether or not I had ever considered the issue. I hesitated for a moment. This was a big question and others around the table were now listening. At the far end of the table Ibrahim, who was originally from the Sudan, spoke up and asked, 'Mark works for the Home Office?'. Adil, a former military surgeon and also originally from the Sudan, was beside Ibrahim and quickly added, 'If Mark's a spy we'll kick him out of here'. I didn't reply to the comments as I didn't really know how and instead, after a moment, returned to my conversation with Victor. Yet, those comments that evening in Kingsburn Hall stood out to me. They were a reminder that the 'immigration line' was always and unavoidably embedded in this research and I could never assume that I had the confidence of others while staying in the shelters. I could not share or fully understand the experience and tragedy of becoming destitute following the refusal of an asylum claim, nor could I assume that I belonged in the shelters simply because I was temporarily living in them for research. As Naveed plainly and politely said to me towards the end of my stay in the shelters: 'at the end of the week you've got a home to go back to. We don't'.

The topic of respect can be an important object of ethnographic study (Bourgois, 2003). Yet, what is not often recognised is the ethnographer's own desire for respect and for assurances from others while conducting research. Feelings of respect can easily bring other gratifying feelings such as comfort and surety. The ethnographer's desire to be respected and assured is also a desire to feel at ease while conducting research. Duneier writes that it is a methodological error to assume that apparent rapport equates to trust (1999: p. 338). This ultimately leads to an unavoidable uncertainty within ethnographic work that must be recognised and declared rather than cloaked behind awkward attempts at methodological resolution. This is the abiding anxiety of any ethnographic work. 'Perhaps the best starting point', writes Duneier, 'is to be aware that a different social position can have a serious effect on one's work, and these differences must be taken seriously' (1999: p. 354). Feeling ill-at-ease or uncertain can have an important role to play in ethnographic research, particularly if it becomes a means to push one out of complacency and recognise the uneven and often concealed tragedies instituted, in the example of my own research, by the processes of bordering.

One evening, early in this research project, I conducted a group interview at the LCC with men staying in the shelter. Carlos and I set up a table in the annex of the church in preparation and invited people to participate. Temir said he was willing to take part but wondered aloud to me why I needed to do the interview as over the past weeks, 'I've already poured my heart out to you'. Temir and two others did participate. However, the consent forms that I produced for the interview immediately became an issue. When I handed one to Temir to read and sign, he asked, 'what the fuck am I meant to do with this?'. The others also looked uncomfortable with the forms. In other contexts, with volunteers and Boaz Trust employees, these were an essential part of gaining what social science researchers call informed consent. It was standard academic practice.

However, for the men staying in the shelters the forms merely exposed the fact that they had nowhere to keep them. They were without a place to call one's own. The consent forms were a material reminder of their destitution and homelessness. My actions, although unintentional, were an afront to their personal dignity. The very documents that were meant to confirm an ethical relationship had become deeply unethical and even shameful. Like my encounter with Wasim at Oxford Road Station, this was a formative moment in my research practice. It revealed how even the most standard social science practices are never completely disconnected from the processes of bordering and that feelings of dignity and indignity, respect and shame will continually emerge in such a politicised context. As Bridget Anderson writes, the term 'asylum seeker' is not simply descriptive of legal status or formal membership, but it is value-laden and negative (2013: p. 4). It is about status in the sense of moral worth and honour. It is a pejorative construction. Drawing on the experiences of the men in the shelter, it's also attached to feelings of shame and dignity and indignity. It's the indignity of not having one's claim for protection believed and it's the shame of not being able to provide for oneself. It's the shame, as both Wasim and Temir's responses to my actions emphasised, of being seen as destitute. It's the grinding indignity of not being able to shower every day or have a choice as to what one eats as one moves from church to church each evening. It is an existence on the edge of the community of value.

One Friday at the Boaz Trust offices, as we waited for transport to the shelter for the night, a hot meal was being served inside the building by another local charity. We stepped inside for the warmth and as we stood in the crowded space, one of the men from the night shelters nudged me and pointed to others queuing for food. 'Mark, don't these people get benefits? Don't they get housing? I bet they waste it all on drugs and alcohol'. On another occasion, as we all sat together in a church, one of the men suddenly told everyone that '80% of people on benefits spend it all on marijuana'. He insisted that we only had to go stand outside the Job Centre in Rusholme to see that this was true. The implication of such statements, and there were many other examples, was that the men staying in the shelters would be good citizens and hard workers, if only given the chance – unlike others around them. Sometimes these divisive statements were aimed at other refugees. When I sat with Adil one evening in the Prestwich Methodist Church, I asked him what his main issues were while living in the shelters. 'There are too many liars, but they have been accepted by the Home Office', he said bluntly. On another evening Victor discussed his thoughts on the asylum system with me. He thought that the Home Office was able to act with relatively impunity as long as it met its targets for reducing immigration numbers and reducing successful asylum claims. As Victor understood it, once a certain quota of refugees had been reached, other asylum claimants would have little hope of gaining refugee status. Izad, a former bodyguard from Tehran, was also in this conversation and agreed with Victor before making reference to a self-immolation that had taken place in the offices of Refugee

Action in Manchester. Izad claimed that a refused asylum seeker from Iran had killed himself in protest at the Home Office accepting too many false asylum claims. Although Izad was not specific about details, he was likely referring to the suicide of Esrafil Shiri who self-immolated in the offices of Refugee Action in 2003 and died of his burns six days later. Reports of Shiri's suicide detail his destitution, ill-health, lack of medical and legal support and fear of returning to Iran (Refugee Action, 2006: p. 19; Kundnani, 2003). Yet, in his own retelling, Izad was adamant that Shiri had done so because too many false claims had been accepted, while Shiri faced the personal humiliation of not being believed. Interpreting Shiri's death in this way may have been a way into understanding Izad's own situation as a refused asylum seeker – a way of making sense of a corrupt system that had rejected him. For Victor and Izad the UK asylum system was a zero-sum game which they had lost to the benefit of dishonest others. These moments and comments are crucial in understanding the community of value not only as a set of deserving and undeserving distinctions emanating from the centre outwards, from the 'good citizen' to the 'immigrant' and 'benefit scrounger', but also as reproduced and redeployed at the fringes of the community of value in order for those who have been excluded to claim legitimacy and maintain a sense of dignity.

Shame is ambivalent, as Lisa Guenther has argued. It is both an indissoluble connection to others and the constant risk that this connection can become afflicting or vexing and that it can become manipulated or exploited. It carries the possibility for both abjection and solidarity. As my encounter with Wasim outside Oxford Road Station indicates, shame can prompt reflection on one's own social situation. It can shake us out of complacency. The ubiquity of modern border regimes means that we are caught up in them whether we realise it or not, whether they are an ever-present factor in our lives or seemingly invisible. To be shaken out of complacency is to realise the tragedy of the border, in all its concealed unevenness.

In this chapter I've tracked some of the different emotions I've encountered while undertaking this research: shame and respect, dignity and indignity, hostility and care among others. They are multi-scalar – ranging from my own feelings and those of others alongside me to the wider emotional landscape that shapes collective identities and ultimately influences how sets of people, like refugees, are viewed and treated. As scholars it seems natural to avoid talking about the emotions of research, as if they cloud our analysis. And yet, through reflective practice of writing – particularly in such a politicised field as migration studies – they can actually reveal so much about us and the contexts we are working in. This requires a shift away from the enchanted ordinary to the translucent ordinary and it requires a recognition that we are situated in the very institutional forms and relational webs that we are working against. It requires a restless justice that does not attempt to mask the complexity or rawness of emotional life, but rather affirm it as a base for new imaginings that work through the deepseated social stratifications and over-determinations of the border.

Notes

1 The allowance available for accessing NASS support was set up to be the equivalent of 70 per cent of Job Seeker's Allowance (Crawley, Price and Hemmings, 2011: p. 8).

2 In more recent years the percentage of refusals has fluctuated. For example, in 2021 67 per cent of initial decisions were grants of asylum (Refugee Council, 2022) while in 2024 63 per cent of initial decisions were refused (Home Office, 2025a). This is, in part, due to the UK Government managing a backlog of asylum decisions. The numbers of applicants awaiting an initial decision rose from 27,000 in 2018 to a peak of 132,000 in 2022. Of these, 88,929 had waited over six months for an initial decision. In 2024 there 91,000 applicants awaiting an initial decision (The Migration Observatory, 2025).

3

The Boaz Trust

For most of its history the offices of the Boaz Trust were located in a former industrial space on Oldham Road, a major transport artery leading into central Manchester that hugs the northern edge of Ancoats. Ancoats is a post-industrial district where regeneration initiatives have left a mix of new-build flats, converted mills, abandoned buildings, wholesalers and trendy bars and restaurants that sit alongside pubs that have seen better days. Directly across from the former offices were a large Post Office sorting house and a cash and carry selling Chinese foods and goods, all of which were a ten to fifteen minute walk from the city centre.

The offices occupied part of the upper floor of the building which centred on a large open area with chairs, tables, a pool table, meeting rooms, PC stations and a kitchen. It was a shared space. The building was owned by Mustard Tree, another faith-based organisation (FBO) which provides support and services to people experiencing poverty and homelessness in the city. The upper floor could be a busy place with those accessing Mustard Tree or Boaz Trust services using the space throughout the day while staff from the Boaz Trust made their way in and out of the dedicated offices located in an enclosed corner section of the floor. The upper floor was used for a variety of activities including well-being classes, English classes, meetings, volunteer training, meals and events. Once every six weeks the Boaz Trust would host a 'Family Night' in the space where visitors, staff, volunteers and those accessing Boaz Trust could meet, share a hot meal, share stories and hear updates and announcements about the organisation. Every Friday evening Mustard Tree would also offer a hot, nutritious meal to visitors in the space. However, to the passer-by, the most prominent and public area of the building was (and remains) the charity shop occupying most of the ground floor. It continues to be run by Mustard Tree and sells furniture, appliances, clothing, electronics and homeware and is staffed by Mustard Tree service users and volunteers including some of the men and women who access Boaz Trust support.

The shared space and overlapping services of the Boaz Trust and Mustard Tree were not only down to their common involvement in homeless support, but also because of their shared history. The Boaz Trust was founded in 2004 by Dave Smith who had also established Mustard Tree eleven years earlier in 1993. The Mustard Tree had its origins in a soup run in Manchester's Chinatown before growing to become a major service provider and support organisation for people experiencing homelessness in the city. It was the increased number of refused and destitute asylum seekers accessing Mustard Tree services at the turn of the Millennium that led Smith to establish the Boaz Trust.

In his 2014 book about the charity, entitled *The Book of Boaz*, Smith writes that the timing of its foundation was linked to the implementation of section 55 of the 2002 Nationality, Immigration and Asylum Act which declared that anyone who did not claim asylum 'as soon as reasonably practicable' after arriving in the UK would not be eligible for National Asylum Support Service (NASS) support (Smith, 2014: p. 43). The 2002 Act privileged 'at-port' claimants over 'in-country' claimants and effectively rendered many irregular migrants, who had not entered the country through official channels, destitute following their asylum claim (Squire, 2009: pp. 75–6; Stevens, 2004: pp. 619–22). According to Smith, by 2003 Mustard Tree was receiving 200 visits a week from asylum seekers. This was 60 per cent of all visitors (Smith, 2014: p. 35). More specifically, the Boaz Trust was born from a joint initiative between Mustard Tree and Refugee Services at the British Red Cross which allocated dedicated support to asylum seekers, including food parcels, cash and toiletries, following the introduction of section 55.

Fifteen people accessed this support during its first week in March 2003, which then rose to eighty-five people per week within four months (Smith, 2014: pp. 44–5). The Boaz Trust was formally established the following year. All of this also coincided with the implementation of the UK's dispersal policy, introduced in the 1999 Immigration and Asylum Act, in which asylum seekers were dispersed on a no-choice basis to areas outside London and the South East in order for their claims to be processed and, in most cases, refused. Without access to NASS support and under No Recourse to Public Funds (NRPF), those whose claims for asylum had been refused (and those affected by section 55 restrictions) would often find themselves destitute and on the streets of cities such as Manchester. Accommodation provision was therefore at the core of the Boaz Trust from its outset. According to Smith:

> When we started it was purely a few people in a spare room. Then people started to donate houses. As we grew it became apparent that we also need a night shelter for those who were street homeless so they could be put somewhere immediately.

In 2020, the Boaz Trust managed twenty-one properties and, alongside hosted accommodation with local residents, provided housing for sixty-two people (Boaz Trust, 2018; Boaz Trust, 2020). Prior to the COVID-19 pandemic, up to twelve spaces were available, specifically for men, in emergency night shelters over the winter season. The organisation includes 14 staff members, ranging from Client Support Workers to a Housing Manager. A solicitor is also available to offer legal advice to those accessing Boaz Trust services. What essentially began as hosted accommodation in 'a few spare rooms' in 2004 has expanded to include housing stock, legal support, and a range of well-being activities, language classes and recreational activities as well as active involvement in national refugee justice campaigns and asylum policy research (British Red Cross and Boaz Trust, 2013; Wheeler, 2024). The Boaz Trust also provides £25 a week on prepaid cards to those living in Boaz Trust housing as well as financial support for travel to appointments and certain legal costs such as document translation (Boaz Trust, 2024).

Holistic service in an uncertain environment

'If you were to ask what we do, we are an accommodation provider to asylum seekers and refugees. That's what we do', Project Manager, Lindsay, said during a recorded interview in the small meeting room within the former office area. 'But we offer a lot of services to our clients', she added. 'It can be everything from advocating to get them doctor's appointments, finding them bus fare for things, right through to legal support'. Through the window of the meeting room door the rest of the modest, open-plan office could be seen. There were staff at their desks and on their telephones and a steady stream of visitors were entering and leaving through the front door. The majority of the interviews I conducted with Boaz Trust employees took place in this meeting room and the interviews were sometimes interrupted by urgent telephone calls or a knock on the door with a request that needed immediate attention. It was all a reminder of how busy the charity was on a day-to-day basis.

'As an organisation we really want to look after the whole person', Lindsay continued. She began talking about the Boaz Life programme that had been introduced and has since become an integral part of the organisation's service. The programme is a series of weekly activities designed to improve the well-being, confidence and vocational skills of those accessing Boaz Trust services as well as help with integration into the local community. It includes activities like sewing, English lessons, IT classes and day trips out to local attractions and the countryside. Boaz Life is a component of the wider 'holistic support' that the organisation aims to provide to its clients. Holistic support means offering a tailored service to each person that addresses the specific needs of their situation. This may involve help in accessing basic healthcare, planning travel to Home Office appointments, finding opportunities to volunteer or simply listening to people as they discuss their situation. It also includes a weekly cash allowance and access to a monthly free shop where donations of food and toiletries are made available.

This holistic support is structured around a series of regular meetings between Boaz Trust case workers and clients. Typically, a client is first referred to the Boaz Trust by another organisation based locally such as Freedom from Torture, Refugee Action or Refugee Services of the British Red Cross. If space in Boaz Trust accommodation is available an initial meeting is set up to explain what the Trust can offer and whether it is suitable for the individual. If the offer of support is accepted, then accommodation is provided for up to 12 months. Following this, a one-month review takes place which, as Kevin, a Boaz Trust case worker explained, is focused on well-being and finding out what activities the person is involved in and what they would like to do while being supported by Boaz Trust. 'At this point', Kevin stated, 'we hope they will have brought with them their legal papers so we can assess where they are up to with their case'. Their case may involve lodging an appeal against the refusal of their asylum claim, making a fresh asylum claim or making an application for section 4 support. Reviews are then scheduled every three months with the long-term aim of getting people to a point where they are ready to move on. This may mean moving back into NASS accommodation after making a successful section 4 application or a fresh asylum claim. It could also, potentially, mean being granted refugee status and leave to remain in the UK.

Accommodation, whether in shared housing or with local residents, provides a more stable ground from which a person can navigate the asylum system but, as Lindsay emphasised, the Boaz Trust offers more of a transition rather than a solution. The perfect scenario, as another employee said, is that a client is able to move on with leave to remain in the UK or re-enter the asylum support system. Yet, this perfect scenario does not always play out. Engagement with an antagonistic Home Office and an unpredictable asylum claims process, does not neatly align with the Boaz Trust's capacity to provide twelve months of accommodation and support. People accessing its services may be subject to deportation, detention and the rejection of their asylum appeal. Their cases may remain unresolved after a year. 'Moving on' is not always an option and while many people are able to re-engage with the asylum system and relocate to NASS accommodation, whether in Manchester or elsewhere, or gain refugee status, some leave their Boaz Trust accommodation under the same legal uncertainty they arrived.

'The problem is far bigger than we can ever deal with at the moment', Dave Smith said during an interview. It was a sentiment echoed by other employees who spoke of the 'scale' and 'bloody-mindedness' of it all. It requires managing expectations and needs and avoiding emotional and physical burnout. Moments of joy when a client receives leave to remain the UK are mingled with moments of sorrow. Their work with people living through an institutionally and policy produced crisis oscillates between a sense of achievement and frustration, relief and despair. There is an abiding and ongoing tension between the organisation's capacity and desire to provide holistic support and the wider injustices of an adversarial border regime.

The Boaz Trust night shelters

The Boaz Trust night shelters were established in 2008, four years after the organisation was founded. According to Dave Smith, while hosted accommodation provided twelve to fifteen spaces at any given time and five houses were in use by the Boaz Trust, there remained a 'real problem finding anywhere for men who were often street homeless'. Like much of the Boaz Trust's history and development, the night shelters had a direct link to earlier work by Mustard Tree:

> We [Mustard Tree] carried out a pilot project over one Christmas, because we knew there were a lot of people from the indigenous population with nowhere to go at night. The council found out and told us that we couldn't do it, but we went ahead anyway, as it was Christmas and the courts were not sitting. In the end they could only slap an injunction on us to prevent us doing it again. […] With that experience in mind, we planned to run a Boaz Trust night shelter for up to ten men for six months from November through to the end of April. As those using it would have no recourse to public funds, we figured that the council would not want to close it down, since there was nowhere else for these men to go, either in theory or in practice (2014: p. 90).

In Smith's account, the night shelters existed at the very threshold of the law. They were a response to the immediate needs of destitute men that the Boaz Trust did not have the capacity to house and that the state had abandoned. Despite the previous injunction against Mustard Tree, according to Smith it was the very legal status of the men – without the right to work, remain or access public support – that allowed the shelters to continue to operate in such a grey area. There would be no place for the men to go, apart from the street.

The night shelters not only existed on the periphery of the law, but also on the periphery of the Boaz Trust's holistic service as they sought to address the immediacy of street homelessness among refused asylum seekers. As Luke, who worked as the Night Shelter

Coordinator between 2014 and 2017, explained during an interview, the men staying in the night shelters were not technically Boaz Trust clients. Some would become clients if they moved into Boaz Trust housing and would have access to more long-term forms of support. He added that, in his role as Night Shelter Coordinator, 'there's guys I've only seen once and moved on'. The shelters were spaces of constant arrival and departure with up to seventy men entering and leaving the network over the course of a winter season. Some would stay for only one or two nights while others would live in the shelters for weeks or months depending on their circumstances and opportunities. Some would eventually move into Boaz Trust housing with other asylum seekers or into hosted accommodation that the organisation arranged with local residents. Others might find alternative accommodation through personal contacts or through temporary state support while others might simply return to the street at the end of a winter season. Luke described how men might leave the shelters suddenly, without notice, while others would give deliberately vague reasons such as 'I'm moving to Newcastle to live with a friend' or they might ask to be dropped off at a train station during the early morning return journey to the city centre as they were 'going to London'. Luke suggested that such statements and explanations might serve as covers for all sorts of scenarios, including exploitative situations, as they sought more stable accommodation elsewhere. He also explained that the continual movement of men in and out of the shelters made it difficult to provide any 'moving on' narratives that were so important for measuring success in the homeless support sector and applying for funding grants.

Yet, Luke also stated that he was committed to making sure 'that the accommodation for them, temporarily, overnight, is the best that it can be'. This meant not only working closely with the seven churches and evening drop-in centre in the shelter network but also with other support organisations in the city who could offer tailored and specific services to meet the men's needs. While recognising the transitory nature of the shelters meant that engagement with the men could sometimes be fleeting, the shelters were viewed by employees as a stepping stone beyond mere emergency accommodation. The men had everyday contact with volunteers and were invited to join in well-being activities at the Boaz Trust such as English classes and trips to the countryside or to sites in

Manchester. Leon, who served as the Night Shelter Coordinator until 2014 and had himself claimed asylum in the UK, explained that through these interactions and activities the men could 'build up their confidence again in life so they believe that there is a reason to keeping hoping and keep fighting'. This was a view echoed by other employees who described the shelters as a first step towards stability. As Dave Smith stated in an interview, 'We'd hope it would be a start for the guys to rebuilding their lives'.

However, there was also a recognition of the limitations of the shelters as a form of support. As Lindsay remarked, 'you've got to do the most basic shelter and food before people can become secure and move on. But I can't see how there is stability in going to a different venue every night and being fed by different people every night and then having twelve hours during the day when you can't go anywhere. I can't see how that is stable'. But ultimately, she concluded, the 'Boaz Trust is an organisation that provides stability. It is not where they stay, but in the organisation. We're their "go to people"'.

The ambiguous status of the night shelters, as sites of constant arrival and departure located on the edge of legality with multiple future trajectories for those using then, means they can be characterised as 'spaces of asylum' with all the contradictions that this term entails. Spaces of asylum, as I have argued, are spaces where the legal and social processes of asylum policy are played out. In their offer of emergency support with limited resources, the shelters were full of tensions between movement and fixity, dignity and indignity and potential stability amid long-term uncertainty. They were sites of localised acts of care and support amid a wider system of hostility and neglect. The Boaz Trust night shelters offered reception and welcome to men off the street who had been rejected by the UK Home Office, yet their ability to meet the men's needs was constrained by capacity and resource limitations.

Eschatology and prophetic radicalism in Manchester

In *The Book of Boaz* Dave Smith writes, 'I'm an Evangelical Christian' and immediately follows this by saying, 'at this point you may be tempted to burn the book, but I beg you to bear with me' (2014: p. 37). The assumed negative reaction on the part of the reader to this revelation is most likely linked to Evangelical Christianity's associations with bigotry and social and political conservatism. It also has a long-standing reputation for viewing poverty as an issue of individual moral failing and for treating charity as an opportunity for proselytising. Such criticisms were vividly expressed in the second half of George Orwell's *Down and Out in Paris and London* where he described his experience of street homelessness in inter-war London (1989). In Christian kitchens, basic meals of bread and tea would be offered on condition of church attendance or alongside compulsory prayer. Salvation Army shelters would be run with military-style discipline including strict codes of conduct intending to correct perceived immoral behaviours such as playing cards, swearing or smoking. Christian groups would enter hostels uninvited to preach and sing at destitute, but disinterested men. No doubt these Christians consoled themselves by thinking how brave they had been 'freely venturing into the lowest dens', Orwell wrote with biting antipathy (1989: p. 194).

Such condescending and coercive practices expressed a moral framing of poverty that viewed vagrancy and unemployment as indicative of a person's spiritual weakness and it's no surprise that in the closing paragraph of the book Orwell vowed to never again support the Salvation Army. Teresa Gowan refers to such discourses as 'sin-talk' as they presumed that moral guilt and personal failings lay behind a person's descent into destitution (2010). This led to Christian organisations taking on a patronising combination of charitable assistance and admonition when addressing homelessness. Deeply ingrained in the social history of Protestant Europe and North America, such spiritual rhetoric has only recently given way to more therapeutic, but no less atomistic, discourses of 'sick-talk' that frame poverty as a pathological problem relating to illness and addiction. Frontline charitable services, whether in the form of soup kitchens or night shelters, were treating people as souls to be saved or bodies to be repaired (Gowan, 2010: pp. 47–51; Wright, 1997: p. 216). Under such 'salvationist' (Allahyari, 2000: p. 76) approaches to care, individuals were being cast as disreputable subjects in need of moral discipline and spiritual redemption which ultimately served as an easy substitute to advocating for substantive social and political change. In short, religious organisations have been accused of refusing to separate service provision from conversion efforts with charitable action becoming a buttress to the wider work of evangelising to the poor.

In view of these criticisms, Dave Smith's caution when describing his evangelical belief is perhaps understandable. But such criticisms are also increasingly contested as FBOs like the Boaz Trust eschew salvationist agendas in favour of service provision that emphasises unconditional love, acceptance, respect and dignity. In an interview with Dave Smith I asked what ethics he saw driving the organisation. He replied, after a thoughtful pause, that it was a 'call for justice'. The UK asylum system was 'very unjust' in its treatment of people and the Boaz Trust was guided by the idea of 'welcoming the stranger when our asylum system doesn't welcome them'. This call for justice flowed from his Christian faith. Smith underlined the role it had played in founding the Boaz Trust stating, 'if you did not trust in God, you would always be waiting for the finance before you did anything. On that basis we would probably not have started in the first place, because the people we are dealing with have no recourse to public funds'. This emphasis on faith-informed justice has now been taken up as an organisational value. On its website the Boaz Trust asserts that it is 'restless for justice' and aims to shine a light on injustice, 'especially where people seeking sanctuary are treated unfairly and we will fight to see change happen' (Boaz Trust, 2025).

While the Boaz Trust is first and foremost an accommodation provider, it also maintains a much more expansive mission in which 'people who seek safety in the UK are welcomed here and free to live life in its fullness'. It also intends to 'challenge unjust systems that cause destitution, both locally and nationally'. This restless justice and its accompanying vision of 'welcome' in the face of the vicious policies and practices of the UK asylum system carries an eschatological weight. A theological concept, eschatology is literally 'discourse on last things'. But as liberation theologians such as Gustavo Gutiérrez and Vitor Westhelle have taught us (Gutiérrez, 1988; Westhelle, 2012), rather than being about apocalypse or catastrophe or speculations on time and eternity, eschatology is the putting into practice a vision of the Kingdom of God in the here and now that disturbs the current social orderings of the world (Gutiérrez, 1988: p. 122). It is a welcome to the other and openness to the 'God who is to come' (Gutiérrez, 1988: p. 125) through the creation of 'tangential' spaces in the present (Westhelle, 2012: p. 20) that open new and alternative social and political possibilities. For Gutiérrez, eschatology becomes operative when it comes into contact with contemporary realities and everyday concerns. It is structured as a condemnation-proclamation. It is the denunciation of the existing order alongside an 'annunciation of what is not yet, but will be; it is a forecast of a different order of things, a new society' (Gutiérrez, 1988: p. 136). We can read the Boaz Trust's restless justice as an example of such a faith-based condemnation-proclamation – a challenge to an unjust system by creating an environment of welcome and dignity. This is what Cloke, Thomas and Williams, in their analysis of FBOs in the UK, call a 'prophetic rationale' or 'prophetic radicalism' (Cloke, Thomas and Williams, 2013; Williams, Cloke and Thomas, 2012). It is an engagement with the subversive power of eschatological promise in order to address things as they are with a practical, grounded vision of how they could be.

Adaptations

The development of the Boaz Trust over the years, from distributing supplies in the wake of section 55 of the 2002 Nationality, Immigration and Asylum Act, to becoming an accommodation provider and legal, advocacy and well-being support organisation has meant the Trust has gone through continual adaptation. This is particularly the case with the night shelters which went through many scheduling and service improvements over the course of their history. For much of their operation, the men using the shelters would meet each night at 9.00 pm outside the Boaz Trust offices in Ancoats. Apart from the Friday evenings when the Mustard Tree would be running its soup kitchen from the upper floor, the building would most often be closed. Here they would wait, exposed to the cold and inclement weather, before a minibus or fleet of cars driven by volunteers would pick them up. At this time the city centre would also be undergoing a general shift to a night-time economy as public buildings and the Arndale Shopping Centre closed and restaurants, pubs and bars began to fill with people. This meant a move away from places that were free to access to places that required a consumer position and assumed certain cultural practices such as the consumption of alcohol. For the men using the shelters, alternative spaces would need to be sought out such as train and coach station waiting areas or they might simply walk the streets.

The need for the men to wait until 9.00 pm was a problem recognised by Leon when he served as the Night Shelter Coordinator. During an interview Leon recalled driving down Oldham Road, near the Boaz Trust offices, one Sunday evening on his way to church. It was 6.00 pm and he saw two men standing at the bus stop. Recognising them from the shelters, he pulled over and asked them where they were going. They replied that they weren't going anywhere but instead were 'waiting for the Boaz'. Leon reminded them that the transport to that night's shelter didn't leave until 9.00 pm. They knew this, they said, but did not have anywhere else to go. For Leon, 'this was really, really shocking. You have genuine asylum seekers with nowhere to go. [They were] waiting outside and it was freezing, Mark. It was completely cold and they had to wait there from 6.00 pm to about 9.00 pm at the bus stop'. Leon added that in his work he often saw these kinds of 'scenes'. In this particular 'scene', waiting on the street not only meant seeing out the evening hours with nothing to do, a boredom directly shaped by their social-legal status, but it also took place under the harsh conditions of a cold, winter night.

My interview with Leon took place in the early spring of 2013 and by the following winter the Boaz Trust would restructure the night shelters to include the Friends Meeting House as a nightly 'drop-in' space. Run by the Society of Friends or 'Quakers', the Friends Meeting House is a grand building across from Manchester Central Library and Manchester Town Hall and had previously served as the Sunday night shelter. This not only meant making new arrangements with all the churches in the network as the pick-up point had changed, but it also meant arranging for a new venue to replace the Friends Meeting House. From the 2013–14 winter season onwards the Ashton Church of the Nazarene in Ashton-Under-Lyne in east Manchester joined the network, and like other venues would provide its own set of volunteers, food provision, bedding, and supplies.

The introduction of an evening drop-in centre wasn't the only major change that took place over the course of the night shelters' existence. The 9.00 pm pick-up time typically meant the meals were served in each church around 9.45 pm which was quite late. Following feedback from the men using the shelters, the opening times of the shelters underwent an overhaul and from the 2014–15 winter season onwards the men would be picked up at 8.00 pm and meal times would take place earlier in the evening at around 8.30 or 8.45 pm. Such changes needed to be supported by every church which could be difficult as they often had other community activities taking place before the shelters opened. As detailed in the Chapter 4, the Longsight Community Church, for instance, hosted a Narcotics Anonymous meeting in the building until 8.30 pm. The venues had to adapt their schedules to implement such changes, but often found ways to work around this. It also meant arranging earlier times for the volunteers with the expectation that overnight volunteers would be spending additional time in the shelter.

The Boaz Trust night shelters were in constant transition, working and re-working their practices and structures. The prophetic radicalism that has characterised the organisation over the course of its history is underscored by a capacity for adaption and, as we will see in the following chapter, the everyday work carried out by volunteers. In this respect, restless justice is not an abstract ideal or transcendent principle, but is given meaning through practice. It is political and ethical action that must be revised and concretised constantly and as such is both fragile and incomplete.

4

Volunteering in the night shelters

At 8.00 pm on a Friday evening in February, Keith parks the minibus he is driving alongside the Friends Meeting House in Manchester City Centre. The Meeting House is on a site where the Society of Friends, or Quakers, have had a presence dating back nearly 200 years. The building's neo-gothic front gives way to a lengthy red-brick structure that is not only used for Quaker worship, but is also a multifunctional space that hosts community activities, political meetings and for-hire events. Every evening throughout the winter season it also serves as a drop-in space for up to twelve men as they wait for transport to the next Boaz Trust shelter for the night. Most of the men have been in the Friends Meeting House since 6.00 pm, sharing biscuits and cups of coffee or tea with the volunteers. Conversations take place in the corner while others watch a film on a plasma screen tv or play board games. When Keith arrives, the men say goodbye to the Society of Friends volunteers, who will stay to close up the drop-in space, and follow him to the minibus outside. Depending on traffic it will be a 20- to 30-minute drive to the Longsight Church of the Nazarene (LCC).

Keith is a retirement age man who was born and raised in Longsight and has attended the LCC since his youth. He has volunteered as the minibus driver for a number of years. It's become part of his weekly routine and he looks forward to Friday evenings when he can catch up with familiar faces or meet new people arriving in the shelter. The work brings him joy and each winter he feels a bond develop between himself and the men. For Keith the work is much more than offering charity to people in need. Rather, it is about building relationships and sharing time with others, regardless of their background or social and legal status. In Keith's words, it's about treating others as 'human beings', whoever they are and this is a core part of his Christian faith and practice.

While Keith is picking up the men from the Friends Meeting House, three volunteers arrive at the LCC. They enter through the portacabin annex at the back of the building as a Narcotics Anonymous meeting is drawing to a close in the main hall. The volunteers begin their work by unpacking the shelter supplies from a small storage area and gather together in bundles blankets, sleeping bags, bed sheets, pillows and floor mats for the men to collect when they arrive. Toiletries and towels are also laid next to the shower area and tables and chairs are set up around the space. They are arranged in a cafe style layout for the evening meal, to create an informal but welcoming atmosphere for the men. Dishes, cutlery, mugs and glasses are also brought in from the kitchen and tea and coffee are brewed. They are all set out on a long table at the front of the space. Two large pots with halal chicken curry and rice are also carried in along with apples, oranges and bananas. The meal was provided by Paul and Olivia, a couple who have attended the LCC for around two decades and are active members with leadership roles in the church. They prepared the meal in their home in Burnage, south Manchester, before driving the short journey to Longsight to drop it off. They will pick up their empty pots when they return to the church on Sunday morning. It's one of the three times they are scheduled to prepare the meal over the winter season.

Phillip is the volunteer responsible for running the shelter that evening, He has keys to the church and was the first to arrive and will be the last to leave the next morning. He is a lab technician at a local hospital and in his late twenties. His partner and young daughter attend the LCC with him. He is joined by Maggie and Rita who are both postgraduate students studying at local universities. Maggie is from Yorkshire and is undertaking an MA in theology. She began volunteering while attending the LCC, a church she admired for its community work. Rita is originally from Argentina and has no religious affiliation but began volunteering through friends who attended the LCC. She also volunteers once a week at Refugee Action, a charity that offers support and legal advice to refugees and asylum seekers in the city. For Rita, working the night shelters offers a glimpse of the daily lives of the men she sometimes meets in a more formal context in the charity offices.

At this time, the church is bustling with activity as the Narcotics Anonymous meeting wraps up. Members chat and mingle in the main hall and foyer before exiting through the main entrance. The meeting leaders will stay behind to clean the room and stack away chairs. Although the shelter preparation and the meeting overlap briefly, the two groups remain in separate areas. It is around this time that Keith and the men arrive. Phillip, Rita and Maggie will welcome them. Some of the men will recognise them from the other times they have volunteered in the shelter or from Rita's work at Refugee Action. While many of the men will have been staying in the shelters for weeks or months, others are arriving at the LCC for the first time and will be shown around the building and facilities by Phillip. The men pick up their sleeping gear and take it to the main hall where they lay out their bedding on the floor. Some might go straight to sleep while most will head back to the annex for the meal. Others will take a shower. Carlos also arrives at the shelter. He is on the pastoral team at the church and has responsibility for the night shelter, coordinating the volunteers and supplies over the season and liaising with the Night Shelter Coordinator at the Boaz Trust. Originally from Colombia, he has lived in the UK for over a decade and is an active presence in the Longsight community where he leads youth work activities. Carlos has been involved in the night shelter for five years and had made immediate changes to the service when he started. Previously, the men had lined up at the kitchen counter for meals where volunteers would dish out the food before the men returned to the main hall to eat. However, Carlos asked the volunteers to set the meal on a table with everyone, including the volunteers, sitting together to eat. In this respect, the meals were not so much 'served' as 'shared' and for Carlos this helped create more of a community atmosphere. It eventually led to the cafe style set-up in the church. Carlos will stay for one or two hours to meet the men and volunteers and ensure everything is running smoothly. Although Carlos does not stay overnight, he will be on call in case Phillip or one of the other volunteers need to contact him.

As the meal begins people sit around tables to eat together. Keith also stays for the meal and continues conversations he has been having with the men since picking them up. After, he will return the minibus to the neighbouring African church who let the LCC borrow it every Friday for the night shelter. Following the meal,

Maggie, Phillip and Rita will clear the tables and wash the dishes. Most of the men will go to the main hall. Some will fall asleep while others will stay up listening to music or watching videos on their phones. Around 10.00 pm Phillip will switch off the lights in the main hall, casting the room into darkness except for the glow of various mobile screens. Phillip will have set up his bedding in the main hall too, while Rita and Maggie set up their bedding in the small foyer space near the entrance which has a sliding partition wall to separate it from the main hall. However, the volunteers will stay up for a while in the annex and chat and play cards over cups of tea with the men who are not ready to sleep just yet.

The work of the overnight volunteers continues the next morning. Phillip's alarm will go off at 7.00 am and the volunteers will wake up to prepare a breakfast of toast, cereal, fruit and boiled eggs. Tea and coffee are brewed again as the men begin to wake up. Some will take showers while others will immediately have breakfast in the annex. Others will sleep as long as possible, until they are woken up by Phillip. They will also all bring their bedding to the annex and leave it in a pile. The sleeping bags, mats and pillows will later be put into storage by the volunteers while the pillowcases and bed sheets will be gathered later that afternoon by a volunteer who will do the laundry at home, returning it all on Sunday morning. The three volunteers will clean the church, hoover the floors, put tables and chairs away, wash dishes and pack away supplies. Often some of the men will help with these duties. At around 8.30 am the men will begin to leave and make their way into Manchester centre by bus or on foot. Once the church is clean and the men have left, the building will be locked and at 9.00 am the leaders of the Latin American church who use the building on Saturdays will arrive for their team meeting.

Every night and morning throughout the winter season, similar scenes take place in the six other churches in the night shelter network: Emmanuel Church of England in Didsbury on Monday nights, Heaton Park Methodist Church in Prestwich on Tuesday nights, St. Clements Church of England in Openshaw on Wednesday nights, Mount Chapel in Broughton, Salford on Thursday nights, South Manchester Family Church in Burnage on Saturday nights and Ashton Church of the Nazarene in Ashton-Under-Lyne on Sunday nights. Across the network, which also includes the evening drop-in space at the Friends Meeting House, 300 volunteers are preparing meals, washing dishes, organising volunteer rotas, driving vehicles, doing laundry and sleeping overnight in churches. The churches are spaces of asylum, on the frontline of a crisis facing destitute, refused asylum seekers on the streets of Manchester. They are focal points of community organising and spaces where a restless justice is put into practice through mundane but essential acts of care.

The Boaz Trust night shelters

While the Boaz Trust coordinated the shelters, each church provided its own volunteers, supplies and transport. An important feature of the network's organisational structure, then, was the relative autonomy given to the churches. With volunteers primarily drawn through individual churches rather than the Boaz Trust itself, the volunteers had little or no direct contact with the Boaz Trust and any training and orientation was done at a church level. At the LCC, the recruitment of volunteers was based on those willing and able to stay overnight on a Friday or prepare meals and included church members and a network of their friends, acquaintances, work colleagues and people within the surrounding community. During interviews with night shelter network volunteers, many spoke about learning about the night shelters during announcements in church or hearing about it from friends. Volunteers also spoke about 'being aware' of the Boaz Trust without knowing much about the organisation. Indeed, Rita stated that she only learned that the Boaz Trust was a religious organisation as our interview was taking place, while Joy, a volunteer at the Saturday shelter said that her only, very indirect, contact with the Boaz Trust had been during a 'sleep-out' protest in support of asylum seeker and refugee destitution in front of the University of Manchester Student's Union. All of this meant that a variety of motivations and experiences were at work among individuals and different practices emerged within each shelter as they utilised their unique spaces.

Like the LCC, the Heaton Park Methodist shelter, Mount Chapel shelter and Kingsburn Hall shelter were all based in purpose-built church halls which eschewed traditional forms of sacred space that may be found in Roman Catholic, Church of England and Eastern

Orthodox churches. Night shelter activities were focused on these halls, although other rooms were also used if space was available. The Emmanuel Church of England shelter was based in a modern two-floor annex to the rear of the nineteenth-century church and had kitchen and shower facilities, a games area, and sleeping areas on the upper floor which were demarcated by mobile wall dividers. The St. Clements Church of England shelter served its meals in a modern foyer, and used a large converted Victorian balcony space as a sleeping area, which also functioned as a storage and activity space throughout the week. The Ashton Church of the Nazarene occupied a former bank and the open area on the ground floor, where worship services would take place, was used to serve meals and socialise, while the former offices on the upper floor were used as separate sleeping areas for the volunteers and men. The buildings that made up the Boaz Trust shelters were designed or retro-fitted to be multi-functional spaces where various activities could take place.

The shelters were often one of many community activities that took place in the churches. The Heaton Park Methodist Church hosted the night shelter on Tuesday evenings, leading to a sometimes rushed 8.30 am exit from the church on Wednesday morning as the building had a short 'turnover' time before a 'Mums and Toddlers' group arrived at 9.00 am. The building manager of the Methodist church explained this to me one morning as the volunteers and men cleared the breakfast tables, washed the dishes, cleaned the hall and packed away shelter supplies before a minibus arrived to take the men back to Manchester city centre. The building manager then pointed towards a schedule pinned to the wall in the first of the church's two ground floor halls. It was a weekly schedule of activities that, alongside church services, included language classes, community choir practices, Sure Start, Zumba!, salsa and other dance classes, Scouts, Brownies, and Alcoholics Anonymous meetings. The Heaton Park Methodist Church had also recently installed a new shower room on the ground floor of the building. I mentioned to the building manager that some of the others staying in the shelters had said it was now the best shower in the network, which he then proudly shared with the other volunteers.

Each shelter also had its own way of organising volunteers with varying numbers of people involved. While in Longsight around seven volunteers would be involved on a Friday night, including a driver, meal preparation and overnight volunteers, at Emmanuel Church of England in Didsbury up to twenty volunteers could be involved, including drivers, a meal team who prepared food in the church, a welcome team to share meals and socialise with the men, an overnight team of two or three volunteers and a morning team who served breakfast and cleaned the venue. At Kingsburn Hall only a few volunteers would be involved in the shelter, like Longsight, while at Heaton Park Methodist Church a welcome team wearing name tags would greet the men and prepare and share the meal with only two or three volunteers remaining to stay overnight.

Each venue also had different sleeping arrangements, based on the space and facilities available in the buildings. At LCC, Kingsburn Hall, Heaton Park Methodist, St. Clements and Emmanuel, the men shared the same space, whether in a large room or church hall, while in Mount Chapel and Ashton Church of the Nazarene the men were able to sleep in separate rooms of two to four people each. The venues also used different spaces around their buildings for different purposes. At the LCC, the church annex became a flexible space that was not only used to serve meals, but also as a social space where people could gather to chat, play games and drink tea and coffee as others slept in the main hall. At Heaton Chapel the main room was used to serve meals while sports highlights and television shows were projected on a pull-down screen along the wall. Later the space could be used for people to socialise as others went to sleep in the adjacent rooms. Such flexibility was a feature across the shelters as churches adapted their spaces to host men overnight.

Theo-ethics and the night shelters

I am an immigrant. A privileged one, to be sure. [...] I live in a community of immigrants. My church consists of as many as 20 different nationalities among around 100 people. Outside the doors of the church are many more – many from Eastern Europe, and many more who have fled the conflicts of Iraq and Syria as well as Somalia and Sudan. Many of them may be called 'legal' immigrants, but many arrived by means outside the official channels seeking refuge from violence and economic ruin at home. Even in our church we have those who came legally and illegally. [...] Our church is a refuge for refugees. During winter months we offer shelter, food, and hot water to homeless asylum seekers left destitute by the government because they have not persuaded the authorities that their cases are genuine. In some cases it is not difficult to discern that there is no danger for them to return home; but in the greatest majority of cases there is only danger and loss and ruin to return to. We don't differentiate in our offer of support between the two cases. God is our judge.[1]

> \- Glenn, LCC shelter volunteer

Glenn is a North American migrant to the UK and a semi-retired academic who is also an ordained minister within the Church of the Nazarene. He has taken up different leadership positions within the LCC over the years and played an important role in establishing links with the Boaz Trust which eventually led to the church joining the night shelter network and opening its building one night a week for refused asylum seekers. Glenn and his family often prepared meals for the night shelter and during a recorded interview with a group of volunteers from the LCC he stated that the church had an obligation to serve the surrounding community and address its particular needs:

It's part of this church particularly that it exists for the sake of the community around it. [...] It's our responsibility to the people who are there. I didn't go out looking for asylum seekers, they came through the door. So, then we realised what the situation was and [asked] 'what do we do?'

In a similar manner, an overnight volunteer named Andy, who was in his mid-thirties and also from a migrant background, stated in a separate interview that, 'I do think that it is important that the churches do outreach, work in the community, help the poor and weakest'. 'From a church point of view', he argued, 'it is whether the church should be insular or doing other things and looking out towards the community. If it's not interacting with or helping the community is there any point in it being there?' Like other churches on the shelter network, as we have seen, the LCC was much more than a place of formal worship. It functioned as a centre for community activities in the area. It was a putting into practice a theo-ethics, where the sacred and the secular, the spiritual and the material combine to form counter-narratives to the prevailing order and its hierarchical social relations. The non-judgemental, unconditional support offered to asylum seekers and refused asylum seekers by the LCC, as articulated by Glenn, is an example of such theo-ethical practice, particularly as asylum seekers and refused asylum seekers have been subject to the UK asylum system's abiding culture of disbelief and denial.

The emergence of the theo-ethical as a concept has coincided with the much wider recognition that faith-based organisations (FBOs), churches and religious groups are increasingly eschewing 'salvationist' approaches to charitable work – in which charity is viewed as an opportunity to convert people – in favour of approaches based on unconditional love, acceptance and dignity. Churches such as the LCC should look outwards and exist for the sake of the community as both Glenn and Andy have suggested and in the next section we will see how such theo-ethical views and practices centre around notions of Christian love or *agape*.

Works of love

I take that word 'justice', not to mean legality. I would take that to mean, in my view, that everybody is made in the image of God and everybody is loved by God and therefore just because somebody happens to be born in a part of the world that is oppressive, it doesn't mean that they should be excluded from the benefits we received.

- Boaz Trust employee

If I'm a Christian and following Christ, his model was people and loving people. He was so big on that. Everywhere in the Bible is about helping your neighbour and loving people. Love is the biggest commandment in the Bible.

- Joy, night shelter volunteer

Over the course of the interviews I conducted with over twenty shelter volunteers and Boaz Trust employees, the notion of Christian love or *agape* would often come up in conversation, particularly when the discussion turned to the role that faith played in their volunteer work or employment and their motivation for working in the night shelters or wider refugee justice sector. During one interview, an employee from the Boaz Trust emphasised how Christian love underpinned the ethical values of the organisation. 'God is love', he said simply and succinctly, 'and he loves the foreigner and those who are displaced and those who are suffering and those who are less well off than us. We're called to do that [love]'. At its most basic, the Christian 'call' to love means to love your neighbour as yourself. This love was the 'biggest commandment' in the Bible, as Joy said during her interview. Joy was a migrant to the UK and originally from Nigeria. She volunteered every Saturday afternoon during the winter months when her church prepared lunch for the men staying in the night shelters.

When Joy talked about the 'biggest commandment' she was most likely referring to the words spoken by Jesus Christ in the New Testament. When asked what the most important commandment within Jewish law was, Jesus replied, 'You shall love the Lord your God will all your heart, and with all your soul, and with all your mind'. This is the greatest and first commandment. And the second is like it: 'You shall love your neighbour as yourself' (Matthew 23: 37–9).

In his meditations on the commandment to love, the nineteenth-century Danish philosopher Søren Kierkegaard argued that there were no limits to who is one's neighbour because 'one's neighbor is all men, unconditionally every human being' (Kierkegaard, 2009: p. 79). Everyone is made in God's image – or carries 'eternity's mark' in Kierkegaard's words – despite being caught up in a world of stratified and hierarchical social relations (Kierkegaard, 2009: p. 97). To love one's neighbour is to 'become a neighbor oneself' (Kierkegaard, 2009: p. 22). In other words, Christian love is a process – a 'becoming' – rather than a static state of being and it requires continual work and practice. Love is an action, rather than a feeling as the anti-racist, feminist scholar bell hooks writes (hooks, 2001: p. 13). For hooks there can be no love without justice and there can be no justice without love (hooks, 2001: p. 13). The two concepts must fold into one another in practice. The realisation that love is a practice is important, particularly in the context of the night shelters. Volunteers and employees rarely declare aloud their ethics to others, except, perhaps, when asked directly by a researcher during a semi-structured interview. These ethics and theo-ethics are rather embodied in the in the ordinary practices, routines and activities necessary to keep the night shelters open such as preparing and serving meals, setting up the shelter supplies and packing them away, washing up dishes and vacuuming the building and opening the church in the evening and closing it in the morning. For some volunteers the shared evening meals were particularly important. Keith explained that 'when you share food with somebody you share a fundamental experience'. 'Food has an amazing connection with people', he continued. 'It doesn't matter, even if you only talk about the food or what they like, it makes a connection'. Similarly, in his reflections in a church newsletter, Zack, who was an American migrant living in Manchester in his mid-twenties and part of the leadership team of the church wrote:

> As we ate with them [the men in the night shelters], we began connecting with them, sharing laughter and small pieces of our lives together. While some of them kept to themselves, many wanted to be known and recognised as fellow people with names and stories and histories. […] It was humbling to encounter these men who would sleep on a different floor each night. Often while returning home from the night shelter thinking about my interactions with the men, I felt my own humanity and identity had somehow deepened.

These 'connections' over shared meals as described by both Keith and Zack, were grounded in a mutual recognition and a shared sense of common humanity. The most important thing, Keith added during his interview, was not the food itself but 'to be seen as a human being'. In this sense the shared meals were moments of 'becoming neighbour' which took place in a non-judgemental context, entirely different to the antagonism and culture of disbelief within the UK's asylum system that had ultimately shaped the lives of the men staying in the shelters in malign ways. The connections described by Zack and Keith – grounded in Christian love as 'becoming neighbour' – are examples of mobile solidarities that involve dynamic engagements between arriving migrants – including asylum seekers and refugees – and more established residents, while also creating moments of solidarity that collapse such distinctions. Yet, an important aspect of this idea is the temporariness of such acts of solidarity. Mobile solidarities are inherently momentary and can dissolve just as easily as they materialise. It is a sobering reminder that 'becoming neighbour' – articulated here as a practice of Christian love – is a hard and arduous work, particularly when it is up against the sustained and systemic injustice of the asylum system.

Learning from shelter work

Working in the night shelters was also a learning process for many of the volunteers. As Cloke, May and Johnsen write, such 'ordinary ethics' of giving and receiving are also 'didactically worked out' as volunteers bring themselves into contact with others (2013). Creating a non-judgemental space not only means engaging with people with unconditional welcome and meeting them at the point of need, but also learning and building on these encounters. Andy commented,

> I think you gain a lot personally, from interacting and finding out about the situation in a different country then your own. You can find out the situation that got them to where they are, without any media intervention on their stories. Often you can be very surprised. There are very educated guys who have done a lot in their lives and have ended up in a situation through no fault of their own.

Volunteers also often spoke about how difficult and emotionally draining it was to see the conditions the men were living in. Another night shelter volunteer, Lisa, mentioned how hard it was to see men the same age as her dad 'sleeping on the floor' of a church. Volunteering in the night shelters also allowed her to witness and understand the persistent boredom experienced by the men:

> I was struck by how bored they were. I was talking to one guy. It was near Christmas and he said he would normally go and sit in the library but it was shut because it was Christmas. That really struck a chord with me. [...] They can't do anything'.

Volunteering alongside refused asylum seekers, and learning about the situations that many of the men had faced and continued to face, prompted some volunteers to engage in further research about asylum policies in the UK. One volunteer spoke about reading government statistics and policy to better understand the circumstances underpinning the shelters, while for Lisa the experience led to more formal research as her MA dissertation addressed issues of asylum and migration. Volunteers also spoke about how their experience allowed them to speak out against stereotypes and negative views of asylum seekers that came up in everyday conversations. Kate said that, 'people complain about foreigners all the time. To be able to tell some of these stories and try and counteract some of those assumptions [is important]. [...] It's nice to have specific, personal evidence when people speak against it'. Another regular volunteer at the shelter said,

> My grandparents were going on a big rant about it [asylum and 'illegal' immigration] and I was like, 'Have you ever met an asylum seeker, a refugee, an illegal immigrant? Where are you getting this negative impression of people you have never met?'.

In the conclusion to their study on homeless service provision in the UK, Cloke, May, and Johnsen argue that there are multiple reasons and motivations behind individuals volunteering in the sector and that the motivation of volunteers is 'far more complex' than the old stereotype of 'self-righteous-do-gooders' can convey (2013: p. 250) with desires to serve the local community, to learn from the people they are serving, and participate in everyday acts of *agape* coming to the fore. Working in the night shelters also often instigated a critical reflection on the immigration system, and the situations and desperate circumstances it forces some individuals into. It also provoked some volunteers to think about their own experiences as immigrants, or their own family histories. This not only led to reflective moments of identification with the men living in the shelters, but also a clear recognition that the immigration system had the capacity to treat some people fundamentally differently from others. In other words, the 'immigration line' became a key point of reflection for volunteers working in the shelters.

Experiences of migration and the limits of shelter work

> I've also found, that almost unanimously, in my contact with people in the immigration system, they believe the worst of every single person. They are not helpful because they don't believe these people should be here. They've got a whole system that is inherently against anybody coming into the country, right across the board. This is what I have found.
>
> - Glenn

> As an immigrant here, I'm on countless visas. I think I'm on my sixth visa application now and it's just a lot of money and a lot of paperwork. And I'll whinge about it. And when I'm in the middle of the experience, I'll think about it [the night shelter] a lot. It's a slap in

the face. I mean, at least I have the ability to do this. I'm ridiculously lucky in the fact that I have a home to go back to if it doesn't work out here. And also the finances, the means, and every box that they need ticked. It's personally quite convicting to have conversations and hear how spoiled I am sometimes.

- Kate, night shelter volunteer

Perhaps due to the multinational character of the LCC and the surrounding community and wider city, many of the night shelter volunteers that I interviewed were, like myself, either migrants to the UK or had come from migrant backgrounds. This experience had given some volunteers a personal insight into the UK immigration system which allowed for unique reflections on the conditions faced by refused asylum seekers more specifically. As Kate stated in her comment above, although she had spent lots of time and money on 'countless visas', she still somehow felt 'lucky' and 'spoiled' in comparison to the men in the night shelters. The night shelters were a space where the unevenness of the UK border regime became starkly apparent. Kate was originally from the USA and, in the words that Glenn had applied to himself, was a sort of 'privileged immigrant'. Drawing further on her experience, and that of her father, who had immigrated to the USA from India, Kate continued:

My dad was an immigrant from India to the USA. And I've seen how difficult and frustrating that is, even if you have the means, finances and paperwork and the right degree and speak the right language. If that's frustrating for me on this level, how much more frustrating is it if you have all these other barriers, or people just won't listen to you or you can't speak the language or whatever? That was a big thing for me. The personal connection.

Lisa, a night shelter volunteer with mixed Kenyan and British heritage also found a 'personal connection' through her experiences of migration. 'It's [volunteering] is a big part of my life', she said, 'with the refugees in particular. It was more familiar to me because it's more similar to home. A lot of the people are from Africa and around the world and it was something that I was able to relate to a lot more'. Andy also drew on his family background and commented, 'being a second generation immigrant, with my Dad coming over and seeking work – obviously that's different from asylum – but it's interesting about being accepted into this country'.

For volunteers like Glenn, Kate, Lisa and Andy the night shelters not only provided a chance to reflect on their own experiences and family histories of migration, but also on the ways in which border regimes and the UK asylum system in particular, treated some people very differently from others. They were spaces that brought to the fore differential inclusion or the immigration line, in Les Back's words. The night shelters, where refused asylum seekers took temporary refuge, were spaces of asylum cut through with the problem of the 'immigration line'. In this respect, it's no wonder that while volunteers often spoke of love, non-judgemental care and creating connections between themselves and the men staying in the shelters, they also expressed frustration and concern about the minimal support that the night shelters could ultimately provide. For instance, Keith, Andy and Kate all questioned why the night shelters had to close each spring. 'Why does it have to end in April?' Kate asked rhetorically during her interview. 'It's Britain. You're not guaranteed warm weather. I understand that it's a volunteer-based network and might fall apart at certain times in the year ...'. In answering her own question Kate exposed the fragile nature of a network that was so dependent on volunteers and a disparate set of churches across the city. Opening the night shelters throughout the year could put a strain on the resources – human, material, financial – of some churches even though having the shelters open year-round seemed to meet an obvious need for some volunteers. Alongside this, the shelters only appeared to offer the most basic support in the face of the broader problems faced by many refused asylum seekers.

'What we do isn't justice. It's just the bare minimum', Carlos said to me as we left a cafe in the more affluent south Manchester suburb of Didsbury following an interview. 'A floor mat, some sleeping bags, two meals and a roof over your head for the night isn't justice, it's just the bare minimum'. Carlos had taken issue with me raising the notion of 'justice' in relation to the night shelters during the interview and argued that, in his view, offering the bare minimum of support could not be considered something akin to justice. Our conversation continued long after the recording had finished. During the interview Carlos had emphasised that the LCC's work with asylum seekers came to down 'to our Christian beliefs of helping people, whoever they are'. 'At least here [in the shelter]', he said, 'we can care for the very least of their needs'. On one hand, these comments were simply indicative of the multiple and divergent understandings that different people brought to their work in the shelters, but it was also a thoughtful reminder that sometimes the forms of unconditional support being offered can seem inadequate. There are always tensions present on the frontline of the migration crisis when *agape* presses up against wider systemic injustice and mobile solidarities continually form and dissolve. 'Becoming neighbour', like restless justice, as I have described it here, is an always incomplete and speculative action, requiring constant and persistent work.

Note

1 This statement was originally posted by 'Glenn' on a social media platform and is used with permission.

5

Time in the shelter

The waiting room

A member of staff sits in front of a plasma screen at the reception desk to the Friends Meeting House on Mount Street in central Manchester and greets visitors. The screen details the activities taking place in the rooms throughout the building that evening which include the Boaz Trust night shelter drop-in space. Every night of the week, over the course of the winter months between November and April, the Society of Friends (or Quakers) would open its doors between 6.00 pm and 9.00 pm to the men staying in the night shelters, providing a warm, welcoming and safe environment to see out the early evening hours before transport arrived to take them to the next church for the night.

The Friends Meeting House effectively served as a waiting room each evening. Yet, in this context, waiting is much more than the experience of spending up to three hours in a drop-in space in central Manchester. It is waiting as an everyday idleness coupled to the antagonistic and potentially threatening bureaucratic processes of the UK asylum regime. It is both mundane and anxious as people are maintained in a state of prolonged legal and social uncertainty, unable to lead fulfilling lives or plan for the future. Time in the shelter, like time on the street, is a product of the slow violence of the UK asylum system which weaponises time to marginalise, delegitimise and exert control over people who have sought sanctuary in the country.

The Friends Meeting House was a multi-functional space. Arriving at the drop-in centre often meant passing other events such as Quaker meetings, small-scale corporate events or a Socialist Workers Party branch meeting. One particular evening, during my stay in the night shelters, I arrived before the other men. In the room was a small table with flasks of tea, water, biscuits and sandwiches. There were two volunteers who had arranged a set of chairs in a semi-circle around a mobile plasma screen and DVD player. When the men began to arrive, a volunteer switched it on. It was the James Bond film *Quantam of Solace* (Forster, 2008) and it continued to play in the background as more and more men entered the room and mingled over mugs of tea and had conversations between themselves or with the volunteers. Amid this activity of men arriving off the street, a scene flashed up on the plasma screen. While driving through the streets of La Paz, Bolivia, James Bond is pulled over by two police officers. Bond steps out of his Range Rover holding fake identity documents and then proceeds to shoot both Bolivian officers in the head before driving off again. Here was James Bond, not only as an undocumented migrant, but as the fictional Hollywood embodiment of British sovereignty, complete with an extra-judicial 'license to kill'. The screen spectacle contrasted with the concrete circumstances of the drop-in space where men – stripped of their rights – exist on the edge of destitution. It marked out the poles of Giorgio Agamben's politics of the 'ban' with one extreme being a fantasy image of British sovereignty and the other as an ongoing, lived reality on a slide towards 'bare life' – where one is outside recourse to the law but remains under its imposition (Agamben, 1998).

Victor was the first to arrive that evening. He cut a lonely figure as he walked into the room and greeted the volunteers before placing his two full bags – his possessions – along the wall beside a table. He then sat quietly in the semi-circle of chairs that had been laid out as the film began to play. It was his first night in the shelters. About twenty minutes later, Victor let out a deep and anguished sigh. It pierced the room. It was not an attempt to get the attention of concerned volunteers as he remained in a sunken position in his chair, his head lowered, almost facing the floor. Rather, it was a moment of deep and introspective uncertainty. Victor had just spent three nights sleeping rough following weeks living an itinerant life among friends after being released from Harmondsworth Immigration Removal Centre. Now he was entering another unknown and uncertain situation, facing the prospect of spending each night on a strange floor in a strange building among strangers.

Victor's sigh that evening resonated through my research. It exposed a moment of deep anguish in someone who otherwise maintained a friendly, talkative and engaging presence in the always public space of the night shelters. The Friends Meeting House was the first encounter with the night shelters for many of the men, most of whom had arrived directly from the street and with little contact with the Boaz Trust beyond the referral forms exchanged between the organisation and other agencies in the city such as Refugee Action or Freedom From Torture. The Friends Meeting House was a site of transition from the street to the more stable, but still unsettled situation of the night shelters. Those arriving in the night shelters for the first time had little idea what to expect. They were waiting on the unexpected, which was another point of transition along a wider trajectory of displacement, rejection and refusal.

In her work on the temporal uncertainty faced by asylum seekers and immigration detainees, Melanie Griffiths identified four experiential temporalities: a 'sticky time' of bureaucratic waiting attached to an often distant hope in a change of status or circumstance, a 'suspended time' of prolonged stasis and stagnation, a 'frenzied' time of sudden change and the accompanying 'temporal ruptures' which tear into people's imagined time frames and futures (2014: p. 1994). This simultaneous speeding up and slowing down within these experiential temporalities is a feature of what I have termed the weaponisation of time. For Victor, and others, prolonged legal and social uncertainty ran concurrent with moments of frenzied and disorienting change, as people moved from the streets to the shelters. Arriving in the night shelters was another 'temporal rupture' amid a series of moments that may have included dispersal, destitution, detention and arrest.

Adil was a smartly dressed surgeon originally from the Sudan who arrived in the shelters with a similar despair to Victor. He appeared an isolated figure as he sat slouched in his chair, head lowered amid a room of men and volunteers who were talking and drinking tea. I introduced myself to Adil and then introduced him to another man who was staying in the shelters and was also originally from Sudan. Adil immediately brightened up and became involved in a conversation that would continue into the shelter later that night. Like Victor's hopes of becoming an accountant if he were to obtain refugee status in the UK, Adil had hopes for the future and was taking ESOL classes during the day in order to obtain an English language qualification in view of one day working in the NHS. Similarly, Izad, a former bodyguard for a politician in Tehran, arrived at the drop-in for the first time with a look of hopelessness and isolation. He had lived in multiple countries since fleeing Iran, including Japan, and had been working illicitly in the UK before he was severely injured in a car accident. It was an event, compounded by his precarious legal status, that had pushed him into destitution. Izad spoke proudly about his former working life in Tehran, Kanagawa and Manchester. He also spoke about his tense escape from Iran which involved a physical confrontation with his arresting police officer. One evening, as we sat talking in the shelter in Broughton, Salford late into the night after all the others had gone to sleep, Izad put me in a simple arm lock and toppled me off my chair in order to prove that, despite his fragile, post-accident condition he was still skilled in martial arts.

Victor, Adil and Izad would talk of their hopes and achievements with pride. Yet, all entered the shelters as withdrawn and discouraged figures. Not all of the men arriving at the drop-in would pick themselves up as quickly as them. One evening, a young man, originally from Egypt and in his late twenties or early thirties, arrived in the Friends Meeting House. Speaking little English he struggled to communicate with the volunteers or the mainly Farsi speakers who were already waiting in the drop-in space. Visibly nervous, he got up and left and then returned whenever one of the others stepped outside for a cigarette. On one occasion he did not return. As a minibus arrived to take us to the shelter at St. Clements in Openshaw for the night, he was nowhere to be seen. Volunteers and other men searched the building and rooms. We called him on his mobile, but it rang out. Arriving at the drop-in for the first time, the young man had simply opted to walk back out into the Manchester night.

Victor, Adil, Izad and the others around them spent the next few months living in the night shelters where they waited in the Friends Meeting House each evening before moving on to a different venue each night of the week. In these churches hearty meals would be provided by volunteers and sleeping bags, floor mats, air mattresses and blankets would be used to turn a church hall into temporary but safe accommodation for the night. These shelters were at once welcoming spaces of shared meals, social interaction and conversation as well as being spaces of restless movement between different venues throughout the week. They were spaces of asylum, with all the contradictions between welcome and exclusion, care and containment and movement and fixity that this term entails. They were spaces where attempts at care and support clashed with the harsh realities of the UK's asylum and border regime and where the discordant temporalities of waiting, whether a few hours in a drop-in centre or weeks and months in the night shelter network were ultimately shaped by the weaponised time of the asylum system where individuals are often maintained in a temporary status over the long term. Victor and Izad would eventually be offered Boaz Trust housing when spaces became available, although this transition to more stable accommodation did not mean their status as refused asylum seekers had been resolved. They arrived and departed the shelters under the same legal uncertainties with which they arrived.

Two years after his stay in the night shelters, during which time he moved into Boaz Trust hosted accommodation with a local family and then into shared Boaz Trust housing with other men whose asylum claims had been refused, I met with Salah in Manchester city centre. Although he was now in more stable housing, like others who arrived in and departed from the shelters, his status had not changed over the years. This was despite attempts to mount an appeal against the decision to refuse him asylum. The inertia had weighed on him. He mentioned that he had not spoken to other volunteers from the shelters for a long while, adding that as his status had not changed 'there was little to say'. Salah had previously spoken about how the shelters had been an opportunity to build contacts with volunteers and others, as well as overcome his shyness. The isolation he began to feel after leaving the shelters and moving into hosted accommodation had continued. He spoke further about these feelings. Salah had recently attended a filming of the BBC's *Big Questions* in Media City, Salford. Queuing with others before the filming and participating in the studio audience had made him feel 'part of society' again, however brief. Salah, through the punitive workings of the asylum system was caught in a seeming 'eternal present' (Anderson, Sharma and Wright, 2009: p. 6).

Over the past three years Salah had undergone significant shifts in status – from 'international student' to 'asylum seeker' to 'refused asylum seeker' – with the depreciating rights that each entails. These can be loosely mapped on to the uncertain temporalities teased out by Melanie Griffiths, particularly as the goal-oriented 'sticky time' of waiting during the asylum claims process gives way to the 'suspended time' of directionless stasis encountered by the refused asylum seeker. These shifts were, in turn, overlaid with changes in accommodation, from state-backed but privatised National Asylum Support Service (NASS) accommodation, to the prospect of living on the street, to reliance on the Boaz Trust night shelters and housing. Salah's goal was to now re-engage in the appeals process and gather fresh evidence for a judicial review of his case. Effectively, it would mean shifting from the 'suspended time' of stasis back to the 'sticky time' of waiting, which offered the small hope of a change in status, yet also remained firmly within the temporal uncertainty of the asylum claims process. On the edges of the community of value the rhythms of weaponised time – whether through the asylum claims process, or the push into dependency on charitable support – subject individuals to temporalities outside their own control and making, and further entrench the marginalisation of refused asylum seekers who are legally and socially constructed as different from those around them.

In figuring the Boaz Trust night shelters as 'waiting rooms', I do not wish to view them as discrete sites, but rather as sites of transition along wider trajectories that may include time in detention, time on the street, time in NASS accommodation or a potential move into more stable Boaz Trust housing. Yet, these transitions do not necessarily imply a change in status and, while the Boaz Trust shelters were at once spaces of welcome and care, there remained an underlying experience of weaponised time that maintained people in legal uncertainty, with severely depreciated rights, and produced forms of differential inclusion.

Arrivals and departures

Remember this evening we were having a conversation about being alive-dead? Being alive-dead. I said to him [Salah], 'I don't feel alive'. I said, 'Sometimes I have this feeling, I don't feel alive'. So how can I fight, y'know? How can people fight for their life? You are losing everyday hope, everyday faith, everything. It's very hard. It's really hard. But I can't see the future, I really can't. If it goes by planning, the planning I do, I can't really see the future. Because, when you know what to do, you always see the future. When you don't know what to do, you never see the future. Right now, I don't know what to do, so how can I see the future? I know that there is my future, but how can I really show that it's mine?

- Temir

I would last see Naveed in late January 2013. We were both in the Longsight Community Church. Naveed was holding documents for an upcoming appointment with immigration authorities. It was his last chance to 'get papers', he said. Naveed pulled out letters, London-bound train tickets and a tube map and began to meticulously go through his upcoming journey, including train times, the tube stations he would need to use and the travel times between them and, finally, his arrival at the meeting. Naveed was visibly anxious as he talked through his journey. Wasim would later tell me privately that Naveed had begun talking to himself and become remote and withdrawn on the street and in the night shelters. In his mid-sixties and originally from Pakistan, Naveed had spent years living precariously in the UK as an asylum seeker and then refused asylum seeker before arriving at the Boaz Trust night shelters where he spent the next three months sleeping on different church floors. Just like his arrival, Naveed's departure from the shelters would be clouded in legal uncertainty.

Jacob arrived in the shelters in early December 2013. He was a middle-aged man and former state-level civil servant from Zimbabwe and had been living in the UK for 12 years. He had been in a sort of legal and social limbo for over a decade as although the UK would not grant him refugee status, Zimbabwe, under the Robert Mugabe regime, refused to accept any deportations from the UK. Jacob had arrived in the shelters after delays in processing his section 4 application. He had been informed by the Home Office that a decision on his application would be given the day he arrived at the night shelters. He had heard nothing. Jacob explained this all to Victor and me as we sat together one evening in a room in the Friends Meeting House. Jacob said that he found the most difficult part of this experience to be the waiting. The lengths of time for decisions to be made and received were always unknown and, in his words, this led to a 'delayed life'. Victor echoed Jacob's feelings, adding that it was all about power. 'Absolute power absolutely corrupts', he said. According to Victor, when a border enforcement organisation like the UK Visas and Immigration (now UK Border Force) is set up to 'please the government' and meet set targets on asylum, it gains an unaccountable power over the lives of individuals. Victor's observation reflected Pierre Bourdieu's theorisation of 'absolute power' as having the means to exert control over other people's experience of time, making an institution entirely unpredictable by subjecting others to different velocities of waiting, whether through delay and deferral or speed and surprise (Bourdieu, 2000: p. 28). It is a power directly attached to their experiences of living under weaponised time. Victor did not bring up his time in detention during our conversation with Jacob, but he often talked about it with me on other occasions. Like Jacob waiting for his section 4 support, Victor found 'waiting' to be one of the most difficult aspects of being detained. Comparing his experience to that of a criminal, Victor said that while criminals are given sentences and know when they will be released, the asylum seeker is given no sentence if and when they are detained and have no idea when they will be released.

The following day, Jacob would learn that his section 4 application had been accepted and accommodation would be available in Bradford in a day's time. That night we were taken to the Mount Chapel shelter in Broughton, Salford and in the morning a volunteer would drive the men, in his car, to the Boaz Trust offices in a series of return journeys. I was not in the same ride as Jacob and by the time I arrived at the offices he had already left. I quickly realised that there would be no chance to say 'good-bye'. Jacob's stay in the shelters was fleeting. It was only two nights, but these two nights were defined by a dysfunctional bureaucratic process. In this respect, it was similar to the experience of other men staying in the shelters, albeit the length of time spent sleeping on church floors might extend to days, weeks or months. As Shahram Khosravi writes, 'One aspect of migrant illegality is that one's life is unsettled, unpredictable and erratic. Migrant illegality means abrupt and dramatic interruptions in one's life, interruptions such as detention, deportation or simply sudden opportunities to move' (2011: p. 69). Arrival and departure are to be understood in this unsettled context. In the Boaz Trust night shelters, among refused asylum seekers, these terms took on multiple and layered meanings. Arrival and departure were not only the repetitive and routine activities of leaving one shelter each morning and arriving at another in the evening, but are also the more singular moments of first arrival in the shelter network and eventual departure from the network, moments which were themselves defined by much wider processes of irregular migration and claiming asylum.

Those arriving at the shelters could have been released from an IRC or forced to vacate NASS accommodation following the refusal of their asylum claim. They could have exhausted the hospitality of friends. It could have been a combination of these and most often involved time spent living on the street. Eventual departure from the shelter could also have been for a variety of reasons. Someone may have been offered a room in Boaz Trust housing or hosted accommodation, or they could have been offered state support through section 4 of the 1999 Immigration and Asylum Act. In some circumstances, as we will see below, a person left the shelters simply because they closed for the season. Just like arrival, departure is also a moment of transition and this transition is not always attached to a sense of progress or resolution. Jacob's move into state-backed, but privatised, accommodation through section 4 support was a route out of the shelters taken by many men. Rejected, but accommodated with voucher support, section 4 maintains individuals in a state of legal and social abandonment and, as Jacob's move indicates, often requires refused asylum seekers to be dispersed to other cities at short notice. In the unsettled situation of the refused asylum seeker, arrival and departure become blurred amid constant movement, displacement and transition.

I opened this section with a quote from Temir, a refused asylum seeker in his mid-twenties originally from Iraq. Temir spoke of 'being alive-dead'. 'Being alive-dead' was a way of expressing his unsettled and unpredictable life spent in the viscous spatial-temporal zone of the border. Temir had been staying in the Boaz Trust night shelters towards the end of the 2013 winter season and his comments were made during a recorded interview alongside Salah and also Samuel, who was originally from Sri Lanka. It was late on a Friday night in the LCC and the three men were offering their thoughts and opinions on their experiences in the night shelters. Earlier that day Temir had walked for two hours to a solicitor's office where he waited for hours before being told to return in two weeks' time. According to Temir, this would mean his application for section 4 support would be delayed for at least one month. As the shelters were closing in two weeks, Temir was facing the prospect of a fortnight living on the street. While Samuel and Salah had been informed that they would be placed in hosted accommodation by the Boaz Trust after the shelters closed, Temir, who was a recent arrival to the shelters, had been informed that accommodation could not be guaranteed. This weighed heavily on Temir during the interview, and it was in this specific context that he spoke of 'being alive-dead'.

'Being alive-dead' is an existence shaped by legal and social abandonment, where time is weaponised and the future foreclosed to the refused asylum seeker. Like Victor's description of his time spent in detention, and Jacob's 'delayed life' waiting for section 4 support, Temir no longer had agency over his future and the bitter prospect of destitution and a return to the street was a distinct possibility. By repeating, 'I can't see the future', Temir communicated what De Genova describes as an 'enforced orientation to the present' where uncertainty and an inability to make long-term plans lead to anxiety over both the present and the future (De Genova, 2002: p. 422). For Temir, this meant that although he had a presence in the shelters and on the Manchester street, he did not feel he belonged to 'normal' society:

> We are not normal people. We have engaged in so many problems. We engage in so many problems that are not normal at all. [...] People I see every day, they have problems. But it's very far from our problems, y'know. So I see a guy who is in a rush because he's late to meet his girlfriend and he's got some problems with her. I see another guy and he don't have the money because he lost it. And I see somebody else who is crying because their father just died. We don't have these kinds of problems.

Temir's observations of the problems faced by 'normal' people became evidence of his own exclusion from everyday social life, his life on the edge of the community of value. His own problems centred on getting a 'passport' and 'papers' which he described as a fight 'which takes a lot of anger and waiting, but I feel it doesn't exist'. 'A life in exile', Khosravi writes, 'is like being condemned to purgatory, a state between life and death, a limbo between here and there' (2011: p. 74). Temir's description of his external landscape, watching people go about their lives with 'normal' problems – and here we must picture him seeing out the day in Manchester Central Library, Piccadilly train station or walking the streets – becomes a description of his inner landscape. Arrival and departure had collapsed into each other for Temir, an expression of legal and social abandonment, a purgatory between life and death.

The locked room

Kingsburn Hall is a large and very drab building located in Burnage, on Kingsway Road – a major, four-lane transport artery linking south Manchester to the city centre. It's plain architecture and interior design reflects its past as a meeting hall of the Brethren – a socially conservative Protestant sect in the Puritan tradition. The building is now owned by the evangelical South Manchester Family Church (SMFC) and although SMFC worships in the gymnasium of a local high school, it uses Kingsburn Hall as an office space as well as for church and community activities. This included the Boaz Trust night shelter. Every Saturday the doors were opened to men using the emergency shelters and, like other venues on the shelter network, volunteers from SMFC and the surrounding community helped in the shelter by preparing and serving meals, providing transport and sleeping overnight.

The main feature of Kingsburn Hall is its large hall with a gentle sloping floor that leads down to a raised stage. It feels like a theatrical space, but without the seating. In winter, the hall becomes damp and cold. One evening in the shelter a full meal of curry, rice, salad and kofte skewers had been prepared by volunteers and served in the ground floor meeting room on a long table. Some men finished their meals quickly and began preparing their bedding for the night, while others continued to talk around the table. When I entered the hall later, Reza – a former butcher from Shiraz, Iran – had already set out a floor mat, sleeping bag and blankets for me. The bedding was laid out in front of a radiator, directly between Reza and Hoza, a young Kurdish man originally from Iran. Our sleeping bags and blankets fanned out from the heat along the wall. In the large hall most of the men arranged their bedding in this way to keep as warm as possible. However, if clustering next to two or three other people with the dry blast of the radiator was too uncomfortable, men also laid out their bedding in the middle of the hall. Victor did so that night, sleeping in a pile of blankets, a semi-personal space detached from everyone else.

By 11.00 pm, the large hall was warm as the heaters had been on since the shelter had opened. At midnight, with the men now sleeping, or half-asleep, a volunteer came to check the room. Deciding that it was now too hot, he made his way to each radiator, stepping between our sleeping bags, in order to switch them off. The cold and damp quickly returned and the night became uncomfortable. Hoza did not keep us awake with his usual loud snoring, as he didn't sleep that night. No one seemed to. My own blanket and sleeping bag were not enough to keep the cold from running through me, so I got up in the dark to rummage through the sleeping supplies at the entrance of the hall, using the light of my mobile phone to search for more blankets. There were none and I returned with only a thin, spare bed sheet.

In the morning, the volunteers woke us up with a 'good morning' and a gentle nudge, if needed. 'This morning is *not* good!', Hoza replied from within his blankets and wrapped head-to-toe in his sleeping bag. Over breakfast the mood was foul, as we had just spent a sleepless night in the bitter cold. Adil suggested that it would have been better to spend the night on the street. He knew some cafes that were open 24 hours and, while we would not have gotten any sleep, we would at least have been warm. Outside the meeting room, we could hear Hoza and the volunteer argue about the heating with the volunteer saying that he thought the hall had been too hot, before adding that switching the heat off had been a mistake and that it wouldn't happen again. As we left the breakfast table and returned to the large hall to pick up our belongings, Adil turned to me and said, 'Mark, when you write, you need to write about this'.

My point here is not to take issue with the efforts of a volunteer who had given up his Saturday night and Sunday morning to drive a minibus to and from the shelter, serve meals, spend time with the men and sleep overnight in the hall. Rather, it is to highlight how the shelters exist at the sharp end of a politics of abandonment in which the wider tensions within 'spaces of asylum', including the tensions between refuge and restriction, become manifest in day-to-day shelter life.

To live in the shelters is to experience a loss of control over one's daily life and routines, where a person has little control over meal times, sleeping arrangements and the temperature of a room. It is to experience the arbitrary. It filters down from the seemingly capricious bureaucratic process of the asylum system to the minute details of shelter life where individuals have little or no say in meal times, their waking times and smoking and sleeping arrangements – all of which vary from venue to venue. It is also an experience of restlessness. This is understood in two ways. It is 'restlessness' in the sense of continued movement, where the wider experience of displacement across international boundaries and dispersal across the UK permeates down into a daily movement between venues in the Boaz Trust shelter network. This restlessness is the inability to settle into a particular space or have a place to call one's one – a continuous and harried oscillation between arrival and departure. Secondly, and attached to the first, it is 'restlessness' in the sense of sleepless or semi-sleepless nights spent on different church floors.

It is at this intersection of legal-social status and daily shelter life, or the macro and the micro, which are never so distinct, that I wish to situate Adil's imperative to 'write about this'. That specific and frustrating moment following a cold and sleepless Saturday night opens up to wider issues both inside and outside the shelter. It is the meshing together of forced dependency, passivity, restlessness and experiences of the arbitrary, alongside the physical experience of using the shelters as a living space which included the very raw experience of sleeping on different church floors. This intersection of legal-social status and shelter life is also the coming together of multiple temporalities as the weaponised, uncertain time of waiting faced by the refused asylum seeker folds into the cyclical and mundane time of arriving and departing shelters each day. It is where the temporality of legal status meets the temporality of dependency, the whole being framed by a sense of 'incarceration'.

During his interview alongside Salah and Samuel in early 2013, Temir expanded on this sense of incarceration, likening his situation to being in a 'locked room', saying:

> I want to have a shower every morning, but I can't. I want to eat whatever I want, but I can't. I want to have money in my pocket, but I haven't had money in my pocket for a while, so long I can't remember. It doesn't mean that I don't like to work or I'm using drugs or gambling. It's because they don't let me work. That's the problem, y'know.

Importantly, Temir's metaphor of the 'locked room' moves between everyday constraints encountered in the shelters and restrictions based on legal status. His frustration at not being able to shower each day or have a say in the meals he eats quickly slides into frustration over his lack of money and, ultimately, his lack of the right to work. The 'locked room' extends from the minutiae of day-to-day shelter life, where access to showers varied from venue to venue and meals were provided by volunteers, out towards more general limitations on the right to work and right to remain. The lived experience of the shelters, however temporary or extended, becomes a component of the lived experience of the legal-social status faced by refused asylum seekers and, in Temir's experience, they tend to collapse into each other.

Temir was not the only person to utilise the metaphor of incarceration over the course of this research. Following my lunch with Salah in Chinatown two years after he had left the night shelters, which I mentioned in the second section of this chapter, we made our way through St. Peter's Square so that I could catch my tram and Salah could continue on to his bus stop. Standing at the tram stop, and before we went our separate ways, Salah commented that he felt like he had been 'let out of prison' for the afternoon.

I first met Arif in early November 2012, while volunteering in the LCC shelter. It was the evening meal and we were gathered around the tables in the main hall with other volunteers and men. Arif, originally from the West Bank, had spent years as an itinerant labourer on building sites in Spain and France, before arriving in the UK. He had a long greying beard and wore a red winter cap that was an almost permanent feature atop his head. Arif was solitary and very introspective. On the street he tended to drift off on his own and in the shelters he could become very private, often talking to himself and sometimes becoming agitated. Despite being withdrawn, he often repeated his desire to work, to have a home and to find a wife. 'I need a job. I need a home. I need a wife', became a constant refrain and one that vocalised the wide crevice between his everyday desires and the severely truncated opportunities that were available to him.

Like Temir's comment about being 'alive-dead' and being in a 'locked room', Arif's statements reflected fundamental problems attached to legal status. On more than one occasion, I misunderstood Arif's frustrations and took them for more immediate and superficial concerns. Later that winter, in 2013, while managing the LCC shelter, Arif approached me soon after the shelter had opened. As the tables were being set up and bedding laid out, he gripped my arm and said, 'Mark, I need space'. Assuming that he wanted to sleep separately from the others that night, especially as the hall lacked privacy, I suggested to another volunteer that we may need to set up a space in the annex for Arif. To double-check these concerns, I asked another Arabic speaker to see if Arif was ok. After speaking to Arif, he turned to me and shrugged his shoulders to say it wasn't clear what Arif was wanting. Later, Arif again approached me and said, 'I need a job. I need a home. I need a wife. *Insha'Allah*'. He repeated it again at the dinner table to others. His need for space hadn't been a request for some minor adjustments to his sleeping arrangements for the night, but deep-seated issues about work, status and domestic life.

Later that summer, as I walked through Manchester city centre, along Shudehill Road on the edge of the Northern Quarter, I bumped into Arif on the street. It had been four months since the shelters had closed. We shook hands and greeted each other in English and Arabic. Arif said he now had housing, but then gripped my upper arm saying, 'It's no good. It's no good. I need money'. Thinking he was in need of cash, I instinctively pulled out my wallet saying, 'All I've got with me is a fiver'. As I did, Arif stepped back, almost recoiling. He gestured that he didn't want my money. He looked disappointed in me. He was not looking for a handout or a bit of cash. Like the previous misunderstanding, this was not about momentary help, but deep-rooted concerns he wished to express to me. However, this time the fragile line between dignity and indignity had been briefly frayed.

Depreciating rights walk hand-in-hand with destitution and dependency and the severe restrictions faced by refused asylum seekers mean they have, 'no control over their major life decisions' (Blitz and Otero-Iglesias, 2011: p. 666). It leads to the pain of dependency and need to constantly rely on others to meet basic needs. References to the 'locked room' and 'prison' were bound to legal and social status and extended beyond mere descriptions of the night shelters and towards wider issues of idleness, joblessness, and isolation. However, we should always be aware that in deploying this metaphor of incarceration, incarceration remains a very real possibility and very real experience for those staying in the shelters, including Victor who had spent five months in Harmondsworth IRC prior to arriving in the shelters.

The shelters as provisional spaces

When men laid out their bedding in the LCC, it was often in front of the radiators along the wall. Others would take eight of the padded chairs and place them in two rows of four facing each other with sleeping mats and sleeping bags on top to create a makeshift, raised bed. Similar arrangements and placements were made across the night shelters as the men adjusted to these uncomfortable spaces. The sleeping area at St. Clements in Openshaw was a converted balcony area that once overlooked the nave. It was now a children's area and storage space with aluminium heaters mounted along both sides of the room's walls. There was often discussion among the men over how many of the eight heaters should be switched on. It was either a night spent under the constant, dry blast of the powerful heaters or a night that might become uncomfortably cold. Whether open spaces such as church halls or the close-quartered rooms in the upper floor annex of Emmanuel Church of England in Didsbury or the Ashton Church of the Nazarene in Ashton-Under-Lyne, staying in the shelters meant constant negotiation with spaces designed for other purposes. There was little to no privacy with the communal sleeping arrangements and the smells of humans in shared spaces with little or no ventilation would mingle with heat and dryness or cold and damp, depending on the space. There was a near-constant snoring and the glow of several mobile phone screens punctuated the halls and rooms. Music could be heard playing from people's headphones and sometimes late-night conversations would take place with friends and family around the world over Skype, Viber and WhatsApp.

As Salah told me during a recorded interview, 'the shelters are not a place for sleeping'. This restlessness was mentioned by others too. One man showed me how he stuffed wads of tissue paper into his ears each night in order to cut out any noise. Paul, originally from Cameroon, and staying in the shelters in early 2015, said he did not sleep the first three nights after his arrival. It took time to get used to the sleeping arrangements, and usually a person learned to sleep out of exhaustion. Betin, a young Kurdish man who had arrived in the UK from Iran at the age of fourteen, only to have his asylum claim rejected when he became an adult, spoke about a friend who had only recently left the shelters for hosted accommodation. His friend, so used to being woken up each morning at 7.00 am, after a short sleep on a church floor, had woken up at that exact same time again only to realise he was in his own bed and could sleep in. He stayed in bed until the afternoon, catching up on much needed sleep. Betin told the story with a smile, saying that he couldn't wait for the opportunity to sleep in a bed and sleep in. Another young man, who had arrived in the UK from Palestine as a teenager, was away from the Longsight shelter one Friday only to return the next week. During a conversation, while I was volunteering at the shelter, he mentioned that he had spent the previous Friday at his friend's house. He was able to sleep in until 1.00 pm. These accounts of sleeplessness were reflected in my own experience of the shelters. During my stay in the shelters I began to develop my own, awkward sleeping routine. It would include one night of little or no sleep, while the following night I would sleep out of pure fatigue, however uncomfortable I was. This pattern dominated my time in the shelters.

The shelters were spaces of tired and aching bodies. The hard floors, sleeping mats and air mattresses, along with the constant change in venue, could wear the body down. Adil would sometimes say that we would all need Thai massages after leaving the shelters, and he would sometimes follow this up by giving a shoulder rub to someone following a night on the shelter floor. Victor often made comparisons between the shelters and detention centres, and once mentioned that having a bed and access to a gym in detention meant he could at least stay physically fit. In the shelters he was aching and constantly tired and, as he once pointed out to me, combined with the hearty but late meals, his fitness gave way to an expanding waistline. Victor was careful to qualify any comparisons by saying in no uncertain terms would he wish to return to a detention centre and that 'no one should have their freedom taken away'.

Yet restlessness is more than just sleeplessness. It is also the temporality of dependency. It is the constant and destabilising movement between shelters, arriving at and departing from a different venue each day, and rotating through the seven venues each week, all of which is set within a wider, prolonged but harried time of waiting and uncertainty. The shelters could only operate as provisional spaces, located, as discussed in Chapter 3, at the threshold of planning law.

As much as the different venues were designed or retro-fitted to become temporary shelters – whether a church hall, converted balcony or modern annex, they were ultimately not designed for living in. In the Boaz Trust night shelters, restlessness became the cyclical time of rotating through these provisional spaces as the days and nights bled into each other. As one man explained to a volunteer, 'we don't look forward to the weekend like you do'. Public buildings were closed and it did not offer the break from day-to-day working life that those outside the shelters experienced. There were moments that brought this clash of temporalities between shelter life and the outside world into focus. It was the moments when a minibus pulled out of the Friends Meeting House on Mount Street and weaved its way through the city centre as the streets filled with weekend revellers and pub crowds. Through the windows an alternative, different form of city life was on display. It was in the moments when the men would be given bus tickets from Ashton Town Centre on a Monday morning and the bus would fill with commuters as it drove along the A635 into Manchester city centre. As people emptied out of the bus on their way to work the men staying in the shelters would often spend their time idle and on the streets or in public buildings, bookies or a shopping centre as they saw out the day.

Yet, while the shelters were provisional, so too are the statuses of the men who used them. For a person seeking asylum it is waiting for a decisive change of status. For someone whose claim has been refused, it is the expectation to leave the country, waiting to lodge an appeal or apply for section 4 support which effectively maintains a person in a state of legal limbo. The experience of restlessness is also an experience of provisional status and the arbitrary impositions that accompany it. It is the experience of having decisions made about you by a seemingly distant, capricious and dysfunctional bureaucracy that shapes fundamental aspects of your life including the right to remain and the right to work. The cyclical and mundane rhythms of shelter life were the result of determinations of status that pushed people into dependency on others which could easily lead to, and exacerbate, frustration and anxiety.

The 'locked room' was a term used by Temir that I have used to describe the restrictions, frustrations, and isolation felt by those living in the Boaz Trust night shelters. This metaphor of incarceration applied to the degraded social-legal status of 'refused asylum seeker', with all the restrictions that this category entails, as much as it applied to the night shelters in particular. Like the other thematic terms I have used to describe the experience of living in the night shelters – 'the waiting room', 'arrivals and departures' – it crosses the macro and the micro, the day-to-day experience of moving between different venues each night of the week, and the wider processes of bordering that shape and restrict the lives of individuals in vicious ways. In conclusion, I would like to reiterate a point I made at the opening of this chapter; that the night shelters were 'spaces of asylum' that carried all the tensions this term entails. They were spaces of movement and fixity, dignity and indignity, of care, concern and welcome; but also of tiredness, restlessness, and anxiety. Whilst the night shelters were spaces that offered support to those whom the state has abandoned, they also could not escape the same processes of bordering and the fault-lines these processes create between those who hold fundamentally different legal-social statuses.

Conclusion

Border stories

Wasim had a recurring dream. It was an image of a dead donkey. He mentioned this dream a few times during his stay in the Boaz Trust night shelters. He spoke about it with me late one night in the annex of the Longsight Community Church (LCC) long after the other men and volunteers had gone to sleep. It was past midnight and I had decided to stay up for a while in order to get some writing done. Wasim noticed I was awake in the annex and walked into the room. I closed my laptop.

We started talking. Wasim told me that he was going to meet a girl the next day. He had met her while walking the streets of Manchester and they had struck up a conversation and exchanged numbers. The relationship had progressed so far that Wasim was potentially going to move in with her. She had been texting him recently with her expectations for him as her new boyfriend. Wasim was slightly nervous when talking about this with me. It was an opportunity for him to get out of the shelters, but it was also a step into the unknown and it meant becoming dependent on another person.

It was then that he once again mentioned the dream of the dead donkey. The disturbing image often appeared to him in his sleep. This time he gave more background about it. When Wasim was a child and living in the Gaza Strip, he and a friend were playing on a building site. They began throwing debris around from the top of the structure. At one point Wasim took an old plank and threw it off the building. It had nails protruding from it. He didn't see that there was a donkey walking past and the plank landed on the animal, the nails piercing its skin. The donkey bellowed and ran off, the plank embedded in its body. A few days later Wasim was walking on a road nearby and came across the same donkey dead on the roadside. The plank was still attached to the corpse. 'I killed that donkey', he said. 'It still haunts me'.

This would be Wasim's last night in the shelters and reciting the dream marked a point of reflection. He not only seemed to be searching for an answer as to why the donkey still haunted him, but also for a meaning behind his time spent destitute and sleeping on different church floors. Over the next three hours Wasim would talk through different moments of his life with me, the things he had said and done wrong. The moments he felt guilt for, whether in his childhood in Palestine or his later life in the UK. Eventually he concluded that *Allah* must have sent him to the night shelters to teach him a lesson and as a sort of punishment to make up for any past wrongs. Now he had the chance to move on. It was 3.00 am by the time he finished talking. Wasim was still grieving the dead donkey, but it also seemed a stand in for his own lost opportunities and lost time.

In the late autumn of 2016, I joined a group of friends for a meal in one of their homes in Longsight, south Manchester. There were around ten of us and we all attended the LCC that was only a short walk from the house. As a group we came from different backgrounds and had different legal-social statuses. Some were born and raised in Manchester while others, like myself, were immigrants to the UK. Some of us were long-term residents or had become naturalised British citizens while others had claimed asylum in the UK and had either been accepted as refugees and had settled into working life in the city or had been rejected and lived under threat of homelessness, detention and deportation. Most of us, regardless of our immigration status, volunteered at the Friday night shelter at the LCC.

Victor was part of the group who shared the meal together. Three years earlier Victor's own asylum claim had been refused by the Home Office and his uncertain legal status had not changed since then, although he was now living in more stable accommodation through friends and supporters in the refugee justice sector. He was now also a regular volunteer in the shelter and stayed overnight each Friday during that winter season. After the meal had finished

Victor suggested that we walk home together as we were both living in Levenshulme, an area of the city just south of Longsight. I had recently returned to Manchester after a year living in Japan with my partner and the walk was a chance for us to catch up. There was a light rain as we followed the dull, yellowish glow of the streetlights along Stockport Road and passed under railway arches and alongside shops and rows of terraced housing. We talked about friends, family and life. We also talked about the night shelters and the people who had passed through them.

'Do you remember Frankie?', Victor asked me. Frankie had stayed in the shelters in early 2014. He was originally from Rwanda and often sang to himself as he laid out bedding for the night or after waking up in the morning. Frankie had an infectious smile and I began smiling while reminiscing about him with Victor. 'He got his refugee status', Victor said. 'That is fantastic news', I responded. I mentioned that I had last seen Frankie in the offices of Refugee Action in central Manchester while conducting a research interview with a member of staff there. He was standing in the reception area, waiting for an appointment with the charity. He had left the night shelters a few months earlier and it was not common to see someone again once they had left. It was even rarer to hear good news about a person's refugee status.

'Do you remember Mohammed?', Victor then asked. Mohammed was originally from Libya and had also stayed in the shelters in 2014. He was balding and kept his head shaved. I remember Mohammed and his friend setting up a makeshift barber's chair one night in the LCC to trim and shave each other's hair. Mohammed had also picked up illicit work in a cafe in the city and had sometimes asked with concern whether he could make his shift in time the next day after sleeping on a church floor. 'He killed himself', Victor said bluntly. I stopped smiling. Victor explained that Mohammed had been arrested, detained and released multiple times after leaving the night shelters. He had experienced systematic harassment from the UK's border regime. It was an attempt to make him leave the country voluntarily. Comingled with his already precarious legal and social status, Mohammed's mental health deteriorated and he eventually took his own life.

The Home Office does not make the number of suicides or incidents of self-harm within the UK's detention estate public, although data released following a Freedom of Information request by the campaign group No Deportations indicated that there were at least two suicide attempts a day among immigration detainees over the summer of 2018. Another, earlier, Freedom of Information request also revealed that 647 detainees had received medical treatment following incidents of self-harm between January and August 2017 (OHare, 2016; Taylor, Walker and Grierson, 2018; Bulman, 2018). The cruel workings of the UK border regime are often hidden from public view, whether behind the walls of the nation's detention centres or in secretive charter flights leaving the country with deportees.

Only a few months later Victor would be subject to the same cat-and-mouse game of detention and release. He would be arrested, detained and then moved between different Immigration Removal Centres and then be released again. On one occasion Victor was released without warning from Dungavel Immigration Removal Centre in South Lanarkshire, Scotland. It seemed a deliberate attempt to separate him from friends and networks in Manchester. In the spring of 2017, Victor was detained a final time and deported to Nigeria on a charter flight.

In spring 2018 I was once again volunteering at the Friday night shelter. It was nearing the end of the winter season and in a couple of weeks the shelter network would be closing again. Most of the men would be placed in alternative accommodation with the Boaz Trust or had successfully applied for section 4 support. I was sitting with a couple of men as we finished breakfast while others were clearing up their bedding or were taking showers or had already left the shelter. Yusuf was distraught. He had no place to go once the shelters closed. 'The Home Office think I'm from Sudan, but I'm not. I'm Eritrean', he said. 'They don't believe me'. He continued, 'where am I meant to stay? Where am I going to sleep? In a tent? Maybe I should make my tent outside this church. Maybe I should just commit suicide'. Nasir, who was originally from Libya and had been staying in the shelters throughout the winter, was sitting next to Yusuf and interjected, nonchalantly. 'No. Suicide won't help anything. I've tried. Twice, I've tried… Only God will decide when you die'. I was taken aback by the conversation. Not only because of the utter despair and bleakness which with Yusuf spoke, but also how mundane and everyday it seemed to Nasir.

In the film *Remain*, Hoda Afshar documents the lives of the men on Manus Island, Papua New Guinea who had been denied refugee status in Australia after attempting to reach the country via boat (2018). Australia had set up extra-territorial prisons on Manus as well as the Pacific Island nation of Nauru in a bid to reduce people seeking asylum in the country. In 2017 the Supreme Court of Papua New Guinea declared the Manus Island prison to be illegal and it was closed down with detainees either being relocated to the capital Port Moresby or remaining on the island. Those on Manus Island continued to pass their time idle but anxious, unable to make a future in Australia and living in hope of being accepted as a refugee elsewhere. They were stuck in limbo. 'The beauty of this green hell burns to the deepest depth of our souls', says Behrouz Boochani to the camera as he stands near a small waterfall where his friend Kamil Hussain had drowned. Later Afshar films Boochani being held in the arms of another fellow asylum seeker as he stands knee deep in water off the shoreline. Boochani's body is limp and the image evokes the Pieta, a Christian image of suffering and mourning as Mary holds the body of her son Jesus Christ after its removal from the cross. In the film, Boochani's companion slowly loses his grip and his body slips into the waters. It is a powerful image. It is an image of mourning and a reminder of the pain and sorrow of those left on the island with uncertain futures, suspended between inclusion and exclusion, life and death. 'We are hostages', wrote Boochani of his experiences on Manus Island before his escape to New Zealand as a refugee (2018: p. 107). 'We are being made examples to strike fear into others, to scare people so they won't come to Australia' (2018: p. 107). The same can be said of the UK asylum system which is grounded in hostility towards people seeking sanctuary and built on the pillars of dispersal, denial, enforced destitution and the weaponisation of time. These operate alongside threats and practices of arrest, detention and deportation. Yet, these cannot be taken as mere deterrents. They do not prevent people from seeking sanctuary in the UK or leaving the UK voluntarily once they have arrived. Rather, they also function as forms of punishment for the very act of seeking asylum and they shape lives and futures in often cruel ways as the stories of the men staying in the night shelters indicate.

Whose time counts and whose lives count are issues of the 'immigration line', of differential inclusion. Judith Butler writes that part of the problem of contemporary political life is that not everyone counts as a subject which is manifest in not everyone's life being considered grievable (Butler, 2009). The 'differential distribution' (Butler, 2009: p. 24) of grievability marks the contours of uneven social life, of the community of value. This ungrievability, I suggest, is not only about life and death, but also a lack of mourning over lost potential and foreclosed futures. It is about wasted time and lost time. The British philosopher Gillian Rose introduces the notion of 'inaugurated mourning' to describe a grief that comes to know the shape of social and political life (Rose, 1996). It does not remain still or in a state of melancholy, but rather it calls for 'new polity to be founded' and a re-engagement with society in the pursuit of justice (Rose, 1996; Schick, 2012: p. 4). The border stories of the men who stayed in the night shelters and the volunteers and employees who worked to support them are enactments of this inaugurated mourning as a restless justice. They are a condemnation of the present order coupled with a vision of what can be – a vision put into practice at a local level, in the face of national policy, through everyday and often mundane acts of care and solidarity.

Borderlands

In her writings on *La Frontera*, the border between Mexico and the United States, the cultural theorist Gloria Anzaldúa writes that 'a borderland is a vague and undetermined place created by the emotional residue of an unnatural boundary. It is in a constant state of transition. The prohibited and the forbidden are its inhabitants' (Anzaldúa, 1987: p. 3). For Anzaldúa a 'borderland' is the more fluid space that hugs the fixed line of the national border which is set up to 'to distinguish *us* from *them*' (Anzaldúa, 1987: p. 3). It is a no-man's-land where 'illegal refugees' are 'caught between being treated as criminals and being able to eat, between resistance and deportation' (Anzaldúa, 1987: p. 5). My suggestion here is that a borderland is not only an area that surrounds the formal boundary of a nation state, but is essentially a part of all social space where differential inclusion plays out and where legal and social statuses are formed and reformed. *La Frontera* is a borderland and so are the streets of Manchester, a post-industrial city in the North of England.

Borders are dispersed spatial-temporal zones of differential inclusion. They produce uncertainty as they oscillate between acceptance and rejection, approval and denial and subject people to prolonged waiting. For some borders seem inconsequential while others are exposed to enforcement, regulation and an antagonistic bureaucracy. For some borders seem invisible while for others they become a matter of life and death. Borders are a form of concrete abstraction as they carry a symbolic value as sheer lines of distinction between inside and outside, yet at the same time they are more concretely – and precisely – a complex assemblage of policies, practices and institutions that shape and reshape lives in often malign ways. As idealised objects they are seen as a marker of the sovereignty of the nation state and therefore need to be defended and controlled. The UK's asylum system is built on this desire for control which becomes hostility in policy and practice. The border stories of Wasim, Izad, Nasir, Victor, Mohammed and Frankie, as well as others who have passed through the night shelters, bear witness to this systemic antagonism. They are stories of grief and pain, exhaustion and shame but also contain moments of resilience and joy.

In this context, the Boaz Trust night shelters were spaces of asylum, at once sites of displacement, on the fringes of public life and society while also being focal points of community activity where mobile solidarities came into being, however temporary. A key part of this research was the time I spent staying in the night shelters, alongside men whose asylum claims had been rejected and who had been rendered destitute as a result. Time in the shelter also became time on the street as I was able to spend days on the streets of Manchester with some of the men as they saw out each day, waiting for the shelters to open and close, whether by walking the streets or sitting in the Central Library or waiting in the Friends Meeting House. It was during these moments that the crucial notion of the 'weaponisation of time' emerged in my research. The border had a temporal dimension through which the social stratifications of legal and social status took shape. Weaponised time was a bifurcated waiting as men saw out their days destitute and without the right to work while also being subject to an antagonistic and often dysfunctional asylum system which places people in a state of social and legal uncertainty for the long term. Weaponised time is also an experience of unpredictability as the men staying in the shelters could be subject to sudden changes of circumstances, sometimes moving to another city at short notice on account of the UK Government's policy of dispersal. Time in the shelter could be as short as a single day, or last for multiple days, weeks, or months, and to those living in the shelters it was often not clear how long their situation would last. Yet, as I argued in the final chapter, arrival to and departure from the night shelters did not necessarily mean a change in legal status. Time in the shelter and time on the street were clouded with legal and temporal uncertainty. If we consider a borderland to be dispersed across civic space and social life, its expression often takes shape in the temporal differentiations it produces. These differentiations can easily go unnoticed in the day-to-day life of a city. The border can become visible or invisible, malign or benign, depending on who you are and your particular social-legal status. Differential inclusion is a fundamental part of social life, even if it isn't always recognised. Part of the abiding power of the border regime is in its forms of concealment where social marginalisation can take place right alongside us, without necessarily confronting us. Writing about the shelters and the border stories of the men who stayed in them is an attempt to shed light on an often-hidden situation facing people who have been refused asylum in the UK and face destitution on account of their immigration status. It is an attempt to rupture the taken-for-grantedness of the situation, or the acceptance of things as they are, with an alternative vision of how things can be, however faint and hazy.

Towards a restless justice

The Boaz Trust night shelters formally closed on 23 March 2020 as the UK entered its first national lockdown during the global COVID-19 pandemic. It marked the end of twelve years of churches around the city opening their doors as emergency accommodation for destitute men whose claims for asylum had been refused. However, in the wake of the network's closure new forms of support have emerged. In 2023 the Restricted Eligibility Support Service (RESS) was established as a joint initiative between three local charities including the Boaz Trust. Providing practical and legal support to people experiencing homelessness on account of their immigration status, the Boaz Trust provides frontline services to those from outside the EU who are primarily people who have had their claims for asylum refused. Taking the form of 'floating support' and grounded in the person-centred and holistic model that was already being practiced across Boaz Trust services, RESS offers a personalised service that may include a budget for mobile phone credit, funds for interpreters and the translation of key documents relating to asylum cases or appeals as well as food and clothing vouchers. The Boaz Trust's well-being services and activities are also made available to people accessing RESS. Importantly, the Boaz Trust can also signpost people to other services including the Greater Manchester Immigration Aid Unit which provides legal support regarding asylum applications and appeals, as well as applications for section 4 support. In a busy week five or six people might apply to the RESS and like the men who were once staying in the night shelters, accommodation is a priority although options are limited or non-existent. Those accessing the support are often living in informal shelters, couch-surfing with acquaintances and friends, or sleeping in cars. However, in the first year of RESS's operation, the Boaz Trust was able to move fourteen people into section 4 and National Asylum Support Service (NASS) accommodation, seven people into Boaz Trust housing, nine people into other voluntary sector accommodation and eleven people into temporary and emergency accommodation provided by the local authority (2024: p. 12). In all of this, it is clear that while the shelter network has now closed, the issues it addressed have not gone away and the Boaz Trust continues to adapt to the needs of those who have been made destitute by the asylum system. In this sense, there is no neat end to the story of the Boaz Trust night shelters, just as there is often no uplifting closure to the border stories of the men who once stayed in them. Prolonged legal and social uncertainty among people seeking sanctuary is a feature of our border regime and it is within this context that an inaugurated mourning comes into being. It is not a passive reaction to the sorrow and pain of lives cut short or foreclosed futures but is a catalyst for a renewed social and political engagement. It is a mourning that refuses closure and insists on ethical action and solidarity. It is the basis of a restless justice. Much more needs to be said about this, and not least about how we might seek both to expose, but also challenge the ubiquitous inequities of the border, to bring into relief the taken-for-grantedness of the current order and strive for new possibilities that consider the world otherwise. It requires recognition that we are situated in the very institutional forms and relational webs that we are often working against whether as researchers or activists or both. It requires a justice that is not so much a transcendent ideal, but rather a socially embedded and grounded concept; an arduous work that is constantly revised and remoulded in practice. The work of the Boaz Trust and its night shelters was based in such a restless justice. While justice and love provided organising principles around which the Trust's employees and volunteers might challenge the cruelty of the asylum system, here too these concepts were often put into practice in the most mundane ways. In fact, it is often through such apparently mundane, even banal everyday practices – examined here in the work of shelter volunteers, and the interactions between shelter volunteers and the men staying in the spaces – that the pervasiveness of the border may be challenged and the work of justice proceed, even as such practices reveal the ambiguities and contradictions of 'spaces of asylum' and the fragile and, in the end always incomplete, nature of a restless justice.

References

Adu, A, Syal, R and Walker, P (2025) 'Starmer reveals plans to send refused asylum seekers to overseas "return hubs"'. 15 May. https://www.theguardian.com/uk-news/2025/may/15/starmer-trip-labelled-an-embarassment-as-albania-rules-out-asylum-seeker-deal.

Afshar, H (dir.) (2018) *Remain*. https://www.hodaafshar.com/remain-video.

Agamben, G (1998) *Homo Sacer: Sovereign Power and Bare Life*, trans. D Heller-Roazen, Stanford, CA: Stanford University Press.

Ahmed, S (2004) *The Cultural Politics of Emotion*, New York, NY: Routledge.

Allahyari, R (2000) *Visions of Charity: Volunteer Workers and Moral Community*, Berkeley, CA: University of California Press.

Anderson, B (2013) *Us and Them? The Dangerous Politics of Immigration Control*, Oxford: Oxford University Press.

Anderson, B, Sharma, N and Wright, C (2009) 'Why no borders?', *Refuge*, 26(2), 1–18.

Anzaldúa, G (1987) Borderlands/ La Frontera: The New Mestiza, San Francisco: Aunt Lute Books.

Association of Senior Children's and Education Librarians (2015) 'Library leaders across England and Wales confirm the welcome offered to refugees and asylum seekers from public libraries', September. https://ascel.org.uk/news/libraries-extend-welcome-refugees-and-migrants.

Back, L (2007) *The Art of Listening*, Oxford: Berg.

Back, L and Sinha, S (2018) *Migrant City*, London: Routledge.

Balibar, É (2002) 'What is a border?', in Balibar, É *Politics and the Other Scene*, trans. Jones, C, Swenson, J and Turner, C, London: Verso, 75–86.

Bayart, JF (2007) *Global Subjects: A Political Critique of Globalization*, trans. Brown, A, Cambridge: Polity.

Beaumont, J and Baker, C (eds) (2011) *Postsecular Cities: Space, Theory, Practice*, London: Continuum.

Beaumont, J and Cloke, P (eds) (2012) *Faith-based Organisations and Exclusion in European Cities*, Bristol: The Policy Press.

Blitz, BK and Otero-Iglesias, M (2011) 'Stateless by any other name: refused asylum seekers in the United Kingdom', Journal of Ethnic and Migration Studies, 37(4), 657–73.

Bloch, A and Schuster, L (2005) 'At the extremes of exclusion: deportation, detention, dispersal', *Ethnic and Racial Studies*, 28(3), 491–512.

Boaz Trust (2013) *Annual reports and financial statements for the year ending 31 March 2013.*

Boaz Trust (2018) *Report 2018.*

Boaz Trust (2020) *Report 2019/2020.* https://hubble-live-assets.s3.amazonaws.com/boaztrust/redactor2_assets/files/359/Boaz_Trust_2019-20_Report.pdf.

Boaz Trust (2024) *Boaz supporter review: 2023–2024 report.* https://www.boaztrust.org.uk/resources/supporter-review-2023-24-.

Boaz Trust (2025) 'Our story'. https://www.boaztrust.org.uk/pages/15-our-story.

Bohmer, C and Shuman, A (2008) *Rejecting Refugees: Political Asylum in the 21st Century*, London: Routledge.

Boochani, B (2018) *No Friend but the Mountains*, trans. Tofighian, O, Sydney: Picador.

Bourdieu, P (2000) *Pascalian Meditations*, trans. Richard Nice, Stanford, CA: Stanford University Press.

Bourgois, P (2003) *In Search of Respect: Selling Crack in El Barrio*, 2nd edn, Cambridge: Cambridge University Press.

Bowling, B and Westenra, S (2018) ' "A really hostile environment": adiaphorization, global policing and the crimmigration control system', *Theoretical Criminology*, 24(2), 163–83.

British Red Cross and Boaz Trust (2013) *A Decade of Destitution: Time to Make a Change*, Manchester: British Red Cross.

Bulman, M (2018) 'Suicides in immigration detention centres kept "state secret" by Home Office, MPs told', *Independent*, 11 September. https://www.independent.co.uk/news/uk/home-news/immigration-detention-centres-uk-suicides-prison-deaths-home-office-a8533366.html.

Butler, J (2009) *Frames of War: When is Life Grieveable?*, London: Verso.

Cloke, P (2009) 'Geography and invisible powers: philosophy, social action and prophetic potential', in Brace, C, Carter, S, Harvey, D and Thomas, N (eds) *Emerging Geographies of Belief*, 9–29, Chicago, IL: University of Chicago Press.

Cloke, P (2010) 'Theo-ethics and radical faith-based praxis in the postsecular city', in Beaumont, J and Molendujk, A (eds) *Exploring the Postsecular: The Religious, the Political and the Urban*, 223–41, Amsterdam: Brill.

Cloke, P (2011) 'Emerging geographies of evil?: theo-ethics and postsecular possibilities', *Cultural Geographies*, 18(4), 475–93.

Cloke, P, Beaumont, J and Williams, A (2013) *Working Faith: Faith-based Organisations and Urban Social Justice*, Milton Keynes: Paternoster.

Cloke, P, May, J and Johnsen, S (2008) 'Performativity and affect in the homeless city', *Environment and Planning D: Society and Space*, 26, 241–63.

Cloke, P, May, J and Johnsen, S (2013) *Swept Up Lives? Re-envisioning the Homeless City*, Chichester: Wiley-Blackwell.

Cloke, P, Thomas, S and Williams, A (2013) 'Faith in action: faith-based organisations, welfare and politics in the contemporary city', in Cloke, P, Beaumont, J and Williams, A (eds) *Working Faith: Faith-based Organisations and Urban Social Justice*, 1–24, Milton Keynes: Paternoster.

Cohen, S (2011) *Folk Devils and Moral Panics: the Creation of the Mods and Rockers*, London: Routledge.

Courea, E (2024) 'Failed Rwanda deportation scheme cost £700m, says Yvette Cooper', *Guardian*. 22 July. https://www.theguardian.com/politics/article/2024/jul/22/failed-rwanda-deportation-scheme-cost-700m-says-yvette-cooper

Crawley, H, Hemmings, J and Price, N (2011) *Coping With Destitution: Survival and Livelihood Strategies of Refused Asylum Seekers Living in the UK*, Oxford: Oxfam.

Cwerner, S (2004) 'Faster, faster, faster: the time politics of asylum in the UK', *Time and Society*, 13(1), 71–88.

Daly, G (1996) *Homeless: Policies, Strategies, and Lives on the Street*, London: Routledge.

Darling, J (2011) 'Domopolitics, governmentality and the regulation of asylum accommodation', *Political Geography*, 30, 263–71.

Darling, J (2017) 'Forced migration and the city: irregularity, informality and the politics of presence', *Progress in Human Geography*, 41(2), 178–98.

Darling, J (2023) *Systems of Suffering: Dispersal and the Denial of Asylum*, London: Pluto Press.

De Genova, N (2002) 'Migrant "illegality" and deportability in everyday life', *Annual Review of Anthropology*, 31(1), 419–47.

De Genova, N (2007) *Working the Boundaries: Race, Space and "Illegality" in Mexican Chicago*, Durham, NC: Duke University Press.

Desjarlais, R (1997) *Shelter Blues: Sanity and Selfhood Among the Homeless*, Philadelphia, PA, University of Pennsylvania Press.

Du Bois, WEB (1989) *The Souls of Black Folk*, New York, NY: Bantam Books.

Duneier, M (1999) *Sidewalk*, New York, NY: Farrar, Strauss and Giroux.

Elgot, J and Taylor, M (2015) 'Calais crisis: Cameron condemned for "dehumanising" description of migrants', *Guardian*. 30 July. https://www.theguardian.com/uk-news/2015/jul/30/david-cameron-migrant-swarm-language-condemned.

Fafinski, M (2021) 'Boris Johnson's roman fantasies'. *Foreign Policy*. 1 November. https://foreignpolicy.com/2021/11/01/boris-johnson-fall-rome-immigration/.

Forster, M (dir.) (2008) *Quantum of Solace*, MGM.

Gill, N (2009) 'Governmental mobility: the power effects of the movement of detained asylum seekers around Britain's detention estate', *Political Geography*, 28, 186–96.

Goodfellow, M (2019) *Hostile Environment: How Immigrants Became Scapegoats*, London: Verso.

Gowan, T (2010) *Hobos, Hustlers and Backsliders: Homeless in San Francisco*, Minneapolis, MN: University of Minnesota Press.

Greenlagh, L and Worpole, K (1995) *Libraries in a World of Change*, London: UCL Press.

Griffiths, M (2014) 'Out of time: the temporal uncertainties of refused asylum seekers and immigration detainees', *Journal of Ethnic and Migration Studies*, 40(12), 1991–2009.

Gromark, S (2013) 'A third wave of receptions: space as concrete abstraction – Łukasz Stanek on Henri Lefebvre', *Site*, 33, 245–52.

Guenther, L (2011) 'Shame and the temporality of social life', *Continental Philosophy Review*, 44, 23–39.

Gutiérrez, G (1988) *A Theology of Liberation: History, Politics, and Salvation*, Sister Inda, C and Eagleson, J (trans. and eds), 15th Anniversary Edition, New York, NY: Orbis Books.

Hanson, S and Rainey, M (2020) 'Towards a contemporary concrete abstract', in Leary-Owhin, ME and McCarthy, JP (eds) *The Routledge Handbook of Henri Lefebvre, The City and Urban Society*, 144–52, London: Routledge.

HM Government (2025). 'Asylum Support'. https://www.gov.uk/asylum-support/what-youll-get.

Home Office (1998) *Fairer, Faster, Firmer – A Modern Approach to Immigration and Asylum*, London: HMSO.

Home Office (2022) *Asylum Support, section 4(2): Policy and Process*. https://assets.publishing.service.gov.uk/media/62ab5278d3bf7f0afd0f8c7f/Section_4_2__policy_and_process.pdf.

Home Office (2025a) 'How many people are granted asylum in the UK?'. https://www.gov.uk/government/statistics/immigration-system-statistics-year-ending-december-2024/how-many-people-are-granted-asylum-in-the-uk.

Home Office (2025b) *Restoring Control of the Immigration System*. https://www.gov.uk/government/publications/restoring-control-over-the-immigration-system-white-paper.

hooks, b (2001) *All About Love*, New York, NY: HarperCollins.

House of Lords (2018) *Impact of 'Hostile Environment' Policy Debate on 14 June 2018*, Policy Briefing, London: HMSO.

Hume, L and Mulcock, J (2004) *Anthropologists in the Field: Cases in Participant Observation*, New York, NY: Colombia University Press.

Hynes, P (2011) *The Dispersal and Exclusion of Asylum Seekers: Between Liminality and Belonging*, Bristol: The Policy Press.

Independent Asylum Commission (2008) *Fit for Purpose Yet?: The Independent Asylum Commission's Interim Findings*. https://www.citizens forsanctuary.org.uk/pages/reports/InterimFindings.pdf.

Jeffrey, C (2008) 'Waiting', *Environment and Planning D: Society and Space*, 26, 954–8.

Johnsen, S, Cloke, P and May, J (2008) 'Imag(in)ing "homeless places": using auto-photography to (re)examine the geographies of homelessness', *Area*, 40, 194–207. https://www.jstor.org/stable/40346114.

Jones, H, Gunaratnam, Y, Bhattacharyya, G, Davies, W, Dhaliwal, S, Forkert, K, Jackson, E and Saltus R (2017) *Go Home? The Politics of Immigration Controversies*, Manchester: Manchester University Press.

Joseph Rowntree Charitable Trust (2007) *Commissioner's Report: Moving on from Destitution to Contribution*. https://www.jrct.org.uk/userfiles/documents/Moving%20On%20-%20from%20destitution%20to%20contribution.pdf.

Kawash, S (1998) 'The homeless body', *Public Culture*, 10(2), 319–39.

Khosravi, S (2011) *'Illegal' Traveller: An Auto-ethnography of Borders*, Basingstoke: Palgrave MacMillan.

Kierkegaard, S (2009) *Works of Love*, trans. Hong, H and Hong, E, New York, NY: HarperCollins.

Kirkup, J and Winnett, R (2012) 'Theresa May interview: "we're going to give illegal migrants a really hostile reception"', *The Telegraph*, 25 May. https://www.telegraph.co.uk/news/0/theresa-may-interview-going-give-illegal-migrants-really-hostile/.

Kundnani, A (2003) 'Destitute Iranian dies after suicide protest at refugee charity', *Institute of Race Relations*. https://irr.org.uk/article/destitute-iranian-dies-after-suicide-protest-at-refugee-charity/.

Leckie, G and Hopkins, J (2002) 'The public place of central libraries: findings from Toronto and Vancouver', *Library Quarterly*, 72(3), 326–72.

Lees, L (1997) 'Ageographic, heterotopia, and Vancouver's new public library', *Environment and Planning D: Society and Space*, 15(3), 321–47.

Lefebvre, H (1991) *The Production of Space*, trans. Nicholson-Smith, D, Oxford: Blackwell.

Lewis, H (2009) *Still Destitute: A Worsening Problem for Refused Asylum Seekers*, York: Joseph Rowntree Charitable Trust.

Lloyd, V (2009) *Law and Transcendence: On the Unfinished Project of Gillian Rose*, Basingstoke: Palgrave MacMillan.

Longsight Community Church of the Nazarene (2016) *Night shelter 2015–2016*, Internal Report.

Longsight Community Church of the Nazarene (2025) 'What we believe'. https://longsightnazarene.org/longsight-community-church-of-the-nazarene/what-we-believe/.

Marcus, GE (1995) 'Ethnography in/of the world system: the emergence of multi-sited ethnography', *Annual Review of Anthropology*, 24, 95–117.

Martin, JC (2020) 'What is a dirtbag Christian?'. 22 October. https://dirtbagchristian.substack.com/p/what-is-a-dirtbag-christian.

Mezzadra, S and Nielson, B (2012) 'Between inclusion and exclusion: on the topology of global space and borders', *Theory, Culture, Society*, 29(4/5), 58–75.

Mezzadra, S and Nielson, B (2013) *Border as Method, or, the Multiplication of Labor*, Durham, NC: Duke University Press.

Migration Observatory (2025) 'The UK's asylum backlog'. 28 April. https://migrationobservatory.ox.ac.uk/resources/briefings/the-uks-asylum-backlog/.

OHare, L (2018) 'At least one person a day is self-harming in UK detention centres', *Independent*. 2 April. https://www.independent.co.uk/news/one-person-a-day-selfharming-uk-detention-centres-a8285206.html.

Orwell, G (1989) *Down and Out in Paris and London*, London: Penguin.

Perraudin, F (2015) 'Diane Abbot: labour's "controls on immigration" mugs are shameful', *Guardian*, 29 March. https://www.theguardian.com/politics/2015/mar/29/diane-abbott-labour-immigration-controls-mugs-shameful.

Phillimore, J and Goodson, L (2006) 'Problem or opportunity? Asylum seekers, refugees, employment and social exclusion in deprived urban areas', *Urban Studies*, 43(10), 1715–36.

Phillips, D (2006) 'Moving towards integration: the housing of asylum seekers and refugees in Britain', *Housing Studies*, 21(4), 539–53.

Philo, C, Briant, E and Donald, P (2013) *Bad News for Refugees*, London: Pluto Press.

Power, N (2014) 'Time does not always heal: state violence and psychic damage', *Open Democracy*. 28 April. https://www.opendemocracy.net/en/transformation/time-does-not-always-heal-state-violence-and-psychic-damage/.

Rainey, MJ (2018) 'Colonus and lampedusa: the tragedy of the border and the dialectics of repair', *Third Text*, 32(1), 150–60.

Rainey, MJ (2019a) 'Time in the shelter: asylum, destitution and legal uncertainty', *Borderlands*, 18(2), 138–64. https://doi.org/10.21307/borderlands-2019-014

Rainey, MJ (2019b) *On the Frontlines of the Migration Crisis: Faith-based Support for Asylum Seekers in Manchester, UK* (多文化世界における アイデンティティと文化的アイコン： 民族・言語・国民を中心に) *Identity and Cultural Icons in a Multicultural World: Ethnicity, Language, Nation*. Hokkaido, University of Hokkaido, 19–34. http://hdl.handle.net/2115/77228.

Refugee Action (2006) *The Destitution Trap: Research into Destitution Among Refused Asylum Seekers in the UK.*

Refugee Council (2019) *Asylum Statistics Annual Trends*. https://www-media.refugeecouncil.org.uk/media/documents/Asylum-Statistics-Annual-Trends-Nov-2019.pdf.

Refugee Council (2022) *Asylum Statistics Annual Trends*. https://www-media.refugeecouncil.org.uk/media/documents/Asylum-Statistics-Annual-Trends-Nov-2022.pdf.

Rose, G (1996) *Mourning Becomes the Law: Philosophy and Representation*, Cambridge: Cambridge University Press.

Rotter, R (2015) 'Waiting in the asylum determination process: just an empty interlude?', *Time and Society*, 25(1), 80–101. https://doi.org/10.1177/0961463X15613654

Rowlands, A (2019) *For Our Welfare and Not Our Harm: A Faith-based Report on the Experience of the Refugee and Refugee Support Community at JRS UK 2017–2019*, Jesuit Refugee Service United Kingdom.

Sartre, JP (2003) *Being and Nothingness*, trans. Barnes, H, London: Routledge.

Schick, K (2012) *Gillian Rose: A Good Enough Justice*, Edinburgh: Edinburgh University Press.

Schuster, L (2005) 'A sledgehammer to crack a nut: deportation, detention and dispersal in Europe', *Social Policy and Administration*, 39(6), 606–21.

Smith, D (2014) *The Book of Boaz or it's Amazing What You Can Do When You Don't Know What You Can't Co!*, Watford: Instant Apostle.

Snyder, M and Hombs, ME (1982) (eds) *Homelessness in America: A Forced March to Nowhere*, Washington DC: Community for Creative Non-Violence.

Squire, V (2009) *The Exclusionary Politics of Asylum*, Basingstoke: Palgrave MacMillan.

Squire, V (2011) 'From community cohesion to mobile solidarities: the city of sanctuary network and strangers into citizens campaign', *Political Studies, 59,* 290–307.

Stanek, Ł (2008) 'Space as concrete abstraction: Hegel, Marx, and Modern Urbanism in Henri Lefebvre', in Goonewardena, K, Kipfer, S, Milgrom, R and Schmid, C (eds) *Space, Difference, Everyday Life: Reading Henri Lefebvre*, 62–79, London: Routledge.

Stanek, Ł (2011) *Henri Lefebvre on Space: Architecture, Urban Research, and the Production of Theory*, Minneapolis, MN: University of Minnesota Press.

Stevens, D (2004) 'The Nationality, Immigration and Asylum Act 2002: secure borders, safe haven?', *Modern Law Review*, 67(4), 616–31.

Stewart, E and Shaffer, M (2015) *Moving On?: Dispersal Policy, Onward Migration and Integration of Refugees in the UK*, University of Strathclyde Glasgow and Economic and Social Research Council. http://migrationscotland.org.uk/uploads/user_contributed/Moving_On_Final_Report_2015.pdf.

Taylor, D, Walker, T and Grierson, J (2018) 'Revealed: two suicide attempts everyday in UK deportation centres', *Guardian*. 11 October. https://www.theguardian.com/uk-news/2018/oct/11/revealed-two-suicide-attempts-every-day-uk-deportation-detention-centres.

Vote Leave (2016) https://www.voteleavetakecontrol.org/.

Walia, H (2013) *Undoing Border Imperialism*, Chico, CA: AK Press.

Walker, P (2021) 'COP26 failure could mean mass migration and food shortages, says Boris Johnson', *Guardian*. 30 October. https://www.theguardian.com/environment/2021/oct/30/cop26-failure-could-mean-mass-migration-and-food-shortages-says-boris-johnson.

Walker, P (2025) ' "Island of strangers" speech echoes of past discordant voices over immigration', *Guardian*. 13 May. https://www.theguardian.com/uk-news/2025/may/13/island-of-strangers-speech-echoes-of-past-discordant-voices-over-immigration.

Westhelle, V (2012) *Eschatology and Space: The Lost Dimension of Theology Past and Present*, New York, NY: Palgrave Macmillan.

Wheeler, W (2024) *A Slow Violence: How Immigration Control Forces People in Greater Manchester into Destitution*. Greater Manchester Immigration Aid Unit and Boaz Trust. https://hubble-live-assets.s3.eu-west-1.amazonaws.com/boaztrust/file_asset/file/935/Destitution_Report_Final_Web.pdf.

Williams, A (2015) 'Postsecular geographies: theo-ethics, rapprochement and neoliberal governance in a faith-based drug programme', *Transactions*, 40, 192–208.

Williams, A, Cloke, P and Thomas, S (2012) 'Co-constituting neoliberalism: faith-based organisations, co-option and resistance in the UK', *Environment and Planning A: Economy and Space*, 44, 1479–501.

Wright, T (1997) *Out of Place: Homeless Mobilizations, Subcities, and Contested Landscapes*, New York, NY: SUNY Press.

Yuval-Davis, N, Wemyss, G and Cassidy, K (2018) 'Everyday bordering, belonging and the reorientation of British immigration legislation. *Sociology*, 52(2), 228–44. https://doi.org/10.1177/0038038517702599

Zetter, R, Griffiths, D and Sigona, N (2005) 'Social capital or social exclusion? The impact of asylum-seeker dispersal on UK refugee community organizations', *Community Development Journal*, 40(2), 169–81.

Index

EU authorised representative for GPSR:
Easy Access System Europe, Mustamäe tee 50,
10621 Tallinn, Estonia
gpsr.requests@easproject.com